The Language of
Colour

LOOK AT THE COLOURS TO THE LEFT . . .

Which one do you identify with most strongly – which one is 'you'?

Which colours make you feel calm . . . secure . . . romantic . . . excited?

Which colours leave you indifferent?

Which one is your 'yuk' colour – the colour you dislike the most?

THE LANGUAGE OF COLOUR

Discover the hidden secrets of colours – how they can help you solve daily problems and project a happy, healthy, and confident image.

About the Author

Dorothee L. Mella is an author, trainer and communications specialist in the field of colour, widely recognised for her development of SICA, the psychological language of colour. As president of Domel Inc., Albuquerque, New Mexico, she is available as a private colour consultant and also offers educational programmes to individuals and groups in government, the private sector and all institutions of learning.

The Language of Colour

Dorothee L. Mella

MICHAEL JOSEPH
London

MICHAEL JOSEPH LTD

Published by the Penguin Group
27 Wrights Lane, London W8 5TZ, England
Viking Penguin Inc., 40 West 23rd Street, New York, New York 10010, USA
Penguin Books Australia Ltd, Ringwood, Victoria, Australia
Penguin Books Canada Ltd, 2801 John Street, Markham, Ontario, Canada
L3R 1B4
Penguin Books (NZ) Ltd, 182–190 Wairau Road, Auckland 10, New Zealand

Penguin Books Ltd, Registered Offices: Harmondsworth, Middlesex, England

First published in Great Britain 1990

Typeset in 11/13 pt Garamond Light by Goodfellow & Egan Ltd, Cambridge
Printed and bound in Great Britain by Richard Clay Ltd, Bungay, Suffolk

A CIP catalogue record for this book is available from the British Library

ISBN 0 7181 3334 X

Many thanks to everyone who gave of
their talents, helped with and experienced
the SICA, the grammar of colour.

Contents

ODE TO COLOUR

Colours are electrons

Visible, they occupy one octave of the
electromagnetic spectrum

To reach you, their rainbow vibrations move
at the speed of light

Yet, they require no medium
for transmission

Learn from your colours, for they are part of you:
mind, eye, and sensation

Use your colours, for they are your personal resource
from the universe

— Dorothee L. Mella

Introduction to the
Self-image Colour Analysis
(SICA)

COLOUR had always been important to me as an artist. But my real interest in colour psychology began in the late 1960s while I was teaching painting at the Maryland School of Art and Design. I was having a particularly difficult time with an advanced painting class because of the unalloyed mix of students, serious artists, hippies, housewives, and three retired military colonels.

It was obvious that there would be a communication problem from the first day I walked into the classroom. There was no interaction among the students. After looking each other over, they were safely entrenched in opposing corners. 'I will listen to you, teacher, if that guy over there will take a bath once a week,' one colonel remarked, typifying the attitudes of the group.

In the midst of my frustration I happened upon a journal kept by the famous abstract artist Wassily Kandinsky. Among his writings, in the *The Art of Spiritual Harmony*, I found a poignant statement: 'Colour acts upon the human body; it is the key touched by man to obtain the appropriate vibration from his creative spirit.' These words inspired me to conduct an experiment with this non-communicative class, using colour as the main medium.

1

With renewed zeal I asked the class to paint a walk in the woods as an introspective exploration using only colour – no representational form: 'Identify your woods with a colour. Make four other colours to harmonise and four more to contrast,' I told them. 'Don't use trees, rocks, or even mountains, use only your colours.' They began their task with excited concentration, oblivious of their classmates for the first time.

When the hour for the final critique of the day arrived, the paintings were placed around the room for all to see. A hush enveloped everyone, except for the same colonel, who broke the silence. 'Hippie, you've been in my woods! Your painting looks exactly like mine! You can't be so bad if you feel the woods as I do.'

I realised there must be some truth to Kandinsky's ideas: colour choice did express an individual's inner feelings. My students' sudden talking and laughing stimulated my determination to continue the colour experimentation.

And I had willing helpers. All the students were excited about what their studies revealed about themselves. We worked with more abstractions. Then we began to develop a colour language that eventually revealed how persons can identify, through individual colour choice, their inner feelings.

The first SICA (Self-image Colour Analysis) was a compilation of forty questions expressing an individual's self-portrait. Questions such as 'What colour represents me?' and 'What colour makes me feel warm, cold, fatigued, happy, sad, etc.?' were correlated for similarities and differences. As eight hundred SICAs were tallied by the art students from among family and friends, the beginnings of a language of colour emerged. Not surprisingly, artists, their families, and their friends readily chose colours to express their moods, desires, and feelings. Others from outside the art profession were more reluctant to express themselves in colour. However, some amazing similarities were discovered among the outsiders. Extroverts and those in expressive professions such as sales selected bright identity colours: reds, oranges, yellows.

Those who relied more upon intuitive and thoughtful abilities in their jobs chose cooler pastel colours for their self-portraits. The colour test and increased self-awareness were put to use in helping students motivate desired change.

How strong an influence colour produced in my life! I searched for credible verification of my findings on the individualised colour responses and colour identities in reference library books, but I found little to substantiate the colour interpretations. My peers in the art society were supportive of what I had stumbled upon, but could not aid in documenting my work.

Then one of my favourite art students, a psychiatrist who was exploring alternative methods of diagnosing his drug-addicted patients, introduced me to *The Luscher Colour Test* by Dr Max Luscher. It was then used by physicians only. I was extremely impressed with his colour test once it had been demonstrated, as I was the one who was examined. My only objection was not directed towards the colour psychology test itself. I felt that there should also be available to the general public a simplified self-portrait method – one where individuals would have the opportunity to choose their *own personal palette* of colours to express their feelings about themselves. And why not an easy colouring system making everyone an artist, in order to portray the average woman and man of society who were wanting only to visualise their positive image and strengths for better communication purposes? Mainly for this reason, I decided to continue on the course of colour study that I had set for myself, that of discovery of a language of colour. (If you're interested in a colour test that gives a scientific and psychological insight into your personality, Dr Luscher's book is still widely available in paperback form today.) Colour had a powerful effect on the life of my psychiatrist friend also, as he was in time to help begin one of the first art therapy departments at a major university in the Washington DC area, which was to explore and teach diverse art forms for self-help.

Rumours about my colour work brought new associates into my life, either to participate in collecting more SICA data, or to inquire if the results of the SICA could solve colour design or colour environmental problems. In response to this interest in colour awareness, I formed a consulting company in 1971 with two co-partners, a sociologist and a design communications specialist. We began consulting and problem-solving in business and government. We offered workshops on colour self-profiling and personal design, and we gave the SICA a new format. We consolidated the number of questions, but the principal ones remained the same ('What colour represents you?' or 'If you could be a colour, what colour would you choose to identify yourself as?' etc). Those who participated in the many colour-painting workshops added more input to the expanding SICA data, since they came from all walks of life – lawyers and government employees alike.

Throughout the years – in tandem with my roles of artist, colour analyst, and colour communications consultant – I have personally served in the administration of over thirty thousand SICAs. My associates have tirelessly gathered information on the beneficial effects resulting from individual and corporate use of the SICA, both for image enhancement and for colours for environmental support. The computerisation of the language of colour, involving many hours of data processing, has enabled us to discover tally-composite colour profiles of many different professional and working peoples. These portraits have given insight into group colour choices, group colour identities, and group 'yuk' colour dislikes – information used for design and image problem-solving needs. Our data excluded economic, racial, and religious information, for we sought only information pertinent to individual preference of colour; and mainly, how one would identify through SICA with oneself.

Now that the colour language has been put on computer, this twenty-year-old art language has been experienced by thousands of people, the meek and powerful alike. The positive results continue to amaze me as I receive letter after letter of thanks attesting to its success.

I have written this book in response to the request of many people who want to analyse their own colour portrait. I feel that SICA can be a tremendous help to individuals, enabling them to know themselves better – an open door to inner communication. We all have the potential to be what we want to be, and often we just require the right tool to help us find the way. Each one of us is an artist in our own special right, creating and communicating ourselves every day. In a world so full of messages and media persuasions, each of us needs a strong sense of our own identity and self-worth. Often our over-stimulating environment prevents us from being able to recognise our own special talent or potential. By achieving this self-recognition we grow in self-acceptance and become more creative in our lives – true contributors to society.

I hope that like thousands of others before you who have experienced the SICA, you will have fun playing with your colours. Take the knowledge and create more power in your life!

Part One

COLOUR,
AN EXPRESSION
OF YOU

1

The Fascination of Colour

THE effects of colour on our minds and bodies is a subject of increasing interest. Scientific studies show that red raises the blood pressure, quickens the pulse, and increases the rate of breathing. Blue, by contrast, slows down body activity and stimulates the mind. These facts, along with other scientific and empirical evidence, are already widely used by the fashion and advertising industries for profit. Ever notice the popular fast-food chains have high-energy colours such as orange in their interiors? Orange is not only a strong appetite stimulant, but it can make the viewer impatient and restless, encouraging the patrons to 'eat and run'. Men always remember the 'woman in red' because that hue is the strongest and longest ray in the visible spectrum, making a greater impression on the retina, not to mention speeding up the emotions! Green, in the middle of the spectrum, has a calming, balancing effect. It can even reduce eyestrain, especially in a minty shade such as the one chosen by hospitals in their operating and recovery rooms. Have you ever noticed a yellow flyer in your advertising papers and junk mail? This stimulating colour was used on purpose to make eye contact – yours – to promote upcoming sales. In many modern office and professional decors there's a popular surge of mauves and violets. Is it a fad, or a revolution – a reaction to the increasing number of sensitive women in the work force? Violets and purples in the sixties were identified with a spiritual-awakening movement. Now, in the eighties, the prevalent use of mauve may reflect a true picture of the intuitive in the workplace. Multiple uses for the psychological uses of colour are becoming more common each day. All are stimulating you, the public, to become more aware of the strong influence of colour energy.

What is colour and why is it important? This fascinating question continues to intrigue us. Colour is reflected light. We feel it and see it through our eyes, our sensory makeup, and our minds. Humans can see 40 percent of the rays of light energy as the visible spectrum, the rainbow of colour. (Many people believe that our sensitivity to colour perception is on the increase as we're listening more and more to our feelings. Tomorrow we may see and perceive colours yet to be recognised by our eyes today.) These vibrations of electro-magnetic energy travel from the sun to reach us. Upon contact, they penetrate our bodies through our eyes and skin – sending instant signals to our brain. When we lie out-of-doors in the sun our bodies absorb light energy. That same energy in a lesser intensity is colour. Colours stimulate an emotional and mental response to what our eyes and bodies record. Strong energy is present in all bright, warm colours, as they are the longest rays of the visible spectrum of light. Not so with the cooler blues and violets or pastel colours, whose intensities are lesser in length and strength. Our brains, the masters of our bodies, respond to each vibratory electron of colour, accepting or rejecting each sensation. Colour, then, is a sensation of light. Colour is a resource of passive solar energy!

Throughout the ages a number of master scientists have attempted to explain the principles of colour and light. Sir Isaac Newton, in the seventeenth century, discovered the visible spectrum and mapped how light breaks into wave-lengths of radiant energy. By producing the first indoor rainbow while directing a beam of light through a prism, he gave science its first major clue in its investigation of the universe. (Duplicating Newton's prism, the modern spectroscope detects the very nature of matter. No other device has performed as accurately in determining the formation of our galaxy.) In his renowned book *Opticks*, Newton arranged his hues to form the original colour wheel, explaining the phenomena of diffraction and interference, or the bending of light. This revealing discovery proved to be the foundation of the science of the physics of light. Where colours were previously used to symbolise the mysteries of the universe, their function could now become the means of revealing them.

The most famous of all modern physicists, Dr Albert Einstein, advanced our space-age awareness with the knowledge and understanding of the complete spectrum of electromagnetic energy – that is, light – how its energy travels through the universe. Without Einstein's genius, measurements of the speed of light and understandings of wavelengths would not have taken place. Our universe can now be explored and realised more fully because of his efforts. Telephones, radios, satellites, X-rays, computers, gamma rays, and cosmic rays, as well as colour, have all become a common part of our lives.

Artists, musicians, and philosophers, such as Da Vinci, Kandinsky, Goethe, Scriabin, Steiner, and Rimsky-Korsakov, have developed theories about the relationship between colour, music, and the inner self. In *The Rainbow Book*, edited by F. Lanier Graham, one can read many connective essays on the ancient and modern physics of the spectrum – light, colour, music, and the stars. One theme flows throughout all hypotheses. Colour is to sight as sound is to hearing; both are vibrational movements of the universe. As energy waves, both are capable of reflection, diffraction, refraction, and interference. Their physical phenomena of intensity, frequency, and wave form create in us our perception of loudness, pitch, and

11

tone in music; and in colour, our awareness to intensity, hue and shade.

Colour has always been honoured with symbolic designations in various cultures through time. We know through hieroglyphic records that the Egyptians placed value on the sun colours. Because of archaeological finds in various parts of the world, we have discovered ancient mystical identities for colours. They represented day, night, birth, life, death, water, and much, much more. Although limited in shades and hues, colours were also favoured to signify man himself; his relationship to his gods, his spirit, his body, his earth, and his actions. An ancient Egyptian papyrus even depicts a healing treatment that prescribed the colour red. In China, the emperor reserved the colour gold for his personal use. The Romans experimented with the 'Pompeii reds'; the Greeks lavished their robes and designs with emerald greens and peacock blues. Was it because the Greeks lived by the sea that they were influenced by oceanic colours; the Romans focused on delight and physical satisfaction, thus the colour red; and the rules of China desired magnificence, as gold expressed power?

To explore all the historical mysteries of colour of each civilisation would fill a book in itself. Colour is one of the most intriguing topics of yesterday. As a subject, it offers investigation into almost every field of study, from mythology, anthropology, and architecture to science, medicine, and psychology. All yield vast sources of information concerning colour uses, sometimes unexplained but always exciting and interesting.

The story of colour is a tale of humankind. Faber Birren's book, *Colour, a Survey in Words and Pictures, From Ancient Mysticism to Modern Science*, offers an excellent account of early cultures' journey through colour history. From the baffling cave drawings of Spain and France, dating back some twenty thousand years, where mineral pigments vividly expressed early hunts, to today's complicated science of laser paintings using light, colour continues to fascinate us.

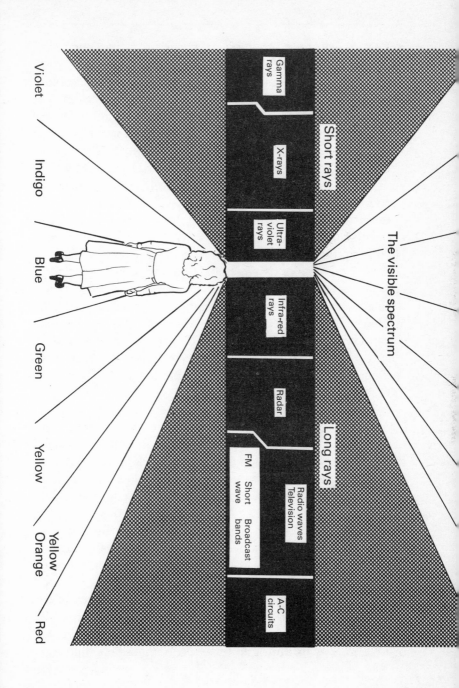

Violet

Indigo

Blue

Green

Yellow

Yellow
Orange

Red

Short rays

Gamma rays

X-rays

Ultra-violet rays

Infra-red rays

Radar

FM Short wave Broadcast bands

Radio waves Television

A-C circuits

Long rays

The visible spectrum

Besides natural phenomena, the earliest paints and dyes were made from nature's organic products. Records from Josephus, the first-century Jewish historian, described blue made from the gemstone lapis lazuli, red from the antlike cochineal insect, and yellow from sulphur soils and chrome minerals. Purple came from seashells, brown from iron clays, white from chalk and lime, while black was made from burnt bones and ivory. These colours were all used by early cultures for pottery, paintings, weaving, home arts, and even decorations for the flesh.

In the nineteenth century pigment dyes took a huge revolutionary step due to the invention of an eighteen-year-old. Henry Perkins discovered aniline dyes, derived from coal tar and carbon compounds, which led the science of chemistry to replace the old organic dye-maker. Modern chemistry now arranges thousands of complex carbon compounds, creating an almost infinite variety of pigment colours.

Varying in tint and shade according to the pigment dye, colours have different energy effects upon us. You may recognise the effect as warm, cool, weak, strong, high, or low. The bright primary colours give higher, warmer, and stronger energy than the soft, weaker, cooler pastels. Some colours are so bright that they create almost an unpleasant effect to our eyes, while others seem so pale that they melt into our skin tones. Some warm us when we're cool, while others bore us with their monotonous repetition. Over and over again, fashion designers advise the proper use of colour to create the right effect.

Not surprisingly, colour response influences many aspects of our lives other than just personal dress. Historical trends in colour may give us a new insight into our culture's emotional state. Articles in the merchandising use of colour in the twentieth century have reported that in the United States since the thirties, there has been a noticeable surge towards reds during wartimes, and more favouring of light blues, greys, black, and browns during times of economic stress. Interestingly, art historians evaluating the mode of dress preceding the French Revolution have noted similarities in the colours and fashions used then to the outfits of the 'flower children' generation of our late sixties.

Colour choice may eventually become a futuristic indicator for people's sentiment during periods of change. Look at blue jeans. They became popular when the youth of America, concerned about the Vietnam conflict, expressed a need for security as well as a desire for more group representation. As the United States assumed more responsibility for its influence around the world, dark blues became the national suit, representing the 'executive'. From the West Coast to the East, the 'punk rock' colours may state a desire to be heard; the mauves declare a need for more sensitivity in the marketplace, and the new bright colour designs of the eighties may express the public's need for more artistic creativity.

Myriad pyschiatric studies have led to the development of art therapy, which uses colour and form to help patients express their hidden emotions and also as a healing tool. As I mentioned in the introduction, one of the better-known tests developed to diagnose patients' emotional condition was created in the late sixties by Dr Max Luscher, a Swiss psychologist. His book, *The Luscher Colour Test*, once intended only for the professional audience, uses colour cards psychometrically in sequential series of choice to reveal a person's psychological makeup.

The recent success of *Colour Me Beautiful* attests to the fact that many people want to understand their personal relationship to colour, as well as needing practical advice on how to use it. The focus of the book was external, offering the reader fashion and beauty advice based on the theory of 'seasonal types' and their most natural flattering colours. I had the great pleasure of meeting the vivacious author of *Colour Me Beautiful*, Carole Jackson, in 1981, when on a consulting trip to northern Virginia. I was honoured, for I felt her book offered a superb colour system for motivation of self-beautification –

one that had helped millions of women and men to look and feel better by matching the correct shades of colour to complexions, eyes, and hair. Her charm and colourful attire portrayed her mastery of her subject matter. Naturally, with our comradeship in the field of colours, she was desirous of experiencing the SICA, which she did. And on my next trip east to teach a ten-week seminar in communicative and self-help qualities of colour, she joined the class. Although extremely knowledgeable of colour fashion, she had become more and more interested in the introspective and self-expressive fields of colour, declaring that she would support my work whenever possible. A year later I was again to meet with this dynamic lady, for she invited me to be her guest speaker at a teaching seminar for her national Colour Me Beautiful consultants. There she presented me with the opportunity of having many of the colour counsellors in attendance experience the SICA. We continue, years later, to travel our parallel courses to support the beautification of the inner and outer worlds of people through colour, as colour remains our medium of communication and exchange.

On the far opposite end of the colour-conscious scale, New Age health practitioners prescribe colours as energy treatments for spiritual and physical alignment and balance. From America's West to East Coasts, there's strong evidence of an increasing demand for the knowledge that these self-help teachers impart. Whatever the theory or practice, each marks a growing insatiable thirst for self-improvement using the common resource of colour.

The Self-image Colour Analysis, SICA, is designed to reveal your intuitive self-portrait. Whatever your favourite colour is today, your personal discernment and colour preference began when you were about two years old. Your likes and dislikes of certain colours have grown and changed with your experiences. As adults, preferences for particular colours are actual information coming from deep within our mental framework. Our colour choices have established a personal language of our feelings – vitality, need, motivation, security, and fulfilment.

The SICA is fun – an inexpensive way of learning about yourself. There are no right or wrong answers. You cannot make a mistake. It will not decide your politics or religion, not even your race or income. The SICA system can only modify for you a non-verbal self-portrait. You can share it or not. But it can show you how you see yourself.

My book will explain exactly how to take the SICA. You'll have fun selecting colours! You may even want to crayon or paint the answers. Imagine yourself an artist who's ready to paint yourself for you and others to see – a wonderfully encouraging self-portrait!

Before you begin your SICA portrait, find a working area where you have ample space and few distractions. Choose a colour for each question asked, or buy a box of twenty-four crayons and lay them out so that all the colours are in full view. Most important, *do not intellectualise* or think too much about each colour selection – spontaneous choice is the key to a more accurate interpretation. Let intuition be your guide! When choosing a colour for each question, select only *one* for each circle. After you have selected all of your colours, you'll be ready to interpret your own image, and just maybe unlock some hidden doors for motivation and self-improvement.

The SICA will be divided into sections, your personal self-portrait and your personal environmental design. The personal portrait will be given first in the beginning of the book. After seeing yourself, you'll be able to select the right colour to wear or design with for the right time or occasion.

You may want to select colours for both the personal and environmental SICA at the same time – do so! If not, do them separately. If for example you desire a quick insight into your image at a certain time, just do your personal portrait SICA. Remember, your colour choices will change as you change, and as you focus on new horizons of yourself, you might even choose a new colour, one you haven't used before. On the other hand, if you only want to change the image or colour decor of your environment, just answer the SICA questions for colours and environment.

You'll find primary rainbow colours, achromatics such as white, black, and grey, as well as basic brown to choose from. Along with these there will even be a choice of gold or silver. Some of you may want more of a variety of colours, but don't worry about selecting the exact shade of the hue, for the more intuitive and spontaneous you are, the more accurate your results will be.

2

Your Self-portrait

YOU are now ready to begin your SICA. The colour analysis will be divided into *two* charts, Charts I and II, to help you visualise the image that you're communicating and how you feel about it. You'll have a choice of *twenty* colours. If you prefer, you can colour in your own circles with coloured pencils, Magic Markers, or crayons. It really doesn't matter how you actually choose your colours – colouring them yourself or selecting them from the colours shown – as long as you choose only *one* colour for each answer. You will receive no extra points for your colouring ability. But have fun and enjoy yourself in whatever way you desire to do the SICA. Of course, you may find the easiest way is simply to choose your colours from the ones displayed on the inside front cover.

Answer each numbered question with a colour! Black, white, grey, brown, silver, and gold are not rainbow hues but are included because they do have colour 'meanings'. I know those of you who are colour sensitive will find it frustrating to be limited to twenty colours, but for the purposes of this book we could not contain *all* colours. The basic colour meaning will *not* change greatly with varying shades or tints. So, if you would prefer a colour not on the selection, try to choose a colour closest to your preferred colour. For example, if you want magenta, choose maroon; but for rust or brick, you will have to choose between orange and brown. And when you interpret your colour choice, just look up both colours for a better understanding of you. For the more hard-to-pin-down colours such as plum, ask yourself, is it more pink or purple? For beige, read brown; for ivory, read white and then yellow for additional insight.

Keep in mind that your colours will change as you change. While your basic self-portrait (your *you* colour) will probably not change a great deal, the other colours will. You might make a colour change the next day. So you should do the test frequently, especially in times of stress.

Remember, try not to be *too analytical*; please be spontaneous! Let intuition and imagination be your guide. Use only one colour for each answer. Read each question carefully; then let a colour come quickly to mind and answer immediately. If you stop to think too much or mull too long over each question, your answers will not be as accurate as they should be. You're the artist, so be intuitive!

RED	LIGHT BLUE
PINK	DARK BLUE
MAROON	MAUVE
ORANGE	PURPLE
PEACH	BROWN
YELLOW	BLACK
MINT GREEN	WHITE
APPLE GREEN	GREY
GREEN	SILVER
BLUE-GREEN (Teal)	GOLD

SICA QUESTIONS

Listed below are the questions for Chart I , and circles 1–7. Each question will have a number corresponding to a numbered circle. Pick your colour for each question asked, and then match it to its corresponding circle. You may *repeat* a colour as often as you like (especially if it's your favourite).

Chart I is designed to portray through the language of colour a portrait of your communicative image; how you see yourself and how others see you. It will provide insight into how you acknowledge yourself, your strengths and those characteristics you like to see in others. Along with people who complement your image, you'll recognise what part of you you prefer not to exhibit. And most important, Chart I will share with you by your colour choices what expands and motivates your communications.

1. *If I were a colour, what colour would I be?*
   (Think of what colour represents you. Don't be concerned about what colour you might wear all the time, but choose a colour that expresses you.)

2. *What colour looks good with that colour?*
   (See a colour that inspires or picks up the colour that represents you.)

3. *What colour unifies those colours to work together?*
   (As a designer what colour would you choose to help your first two colour choices work together in a colour chord?)

4. *What colour harmonises (has something in common) with your number 1 colour choice?*
   (Think of a colour that is complementary or blends well with the colour that represents you.)

5. *What colour contrasts (is different from) your number 1 colour choice?*
   (This colour should be different from, but not in conflict with, the colour that represents you.)

6. *What is your 'yuk' colour?*
   (This is a colour you do not like to wear or have around you in your environment.)

21

SICA SELF-PORTRAIT PART I

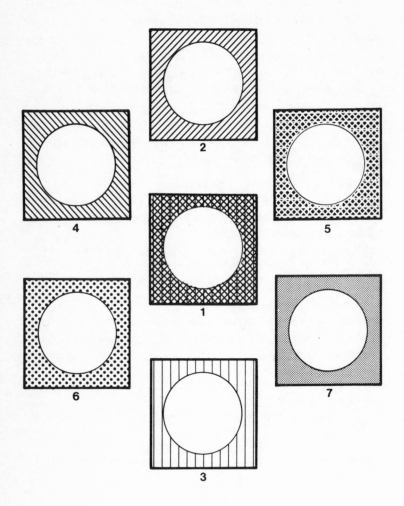

7. *Without looking at your 'yuk' colour (cover it up with your hand), study your colour selections for a moment. What colour motivates all the colours that you have chosen to work or go into action together?*
(This is a colour that unifies your colour choices.)

SICA QUESTIONS FOR CHART II

For Chart II, the questions and circles A–G are designed to help show you how in touch you are with yourself through feeling and sensing. This part of the SICA will give you insight, through intuitive colour choice, into how well you communicate with yourself. In addition you'll learn your areas of stress, or your non-communicative zones, and you'll see what you need for self-enhancement and greater happiness. So be very intuitive with these colour selections! Read the questions and quickly respond with your colour answer for accurate results.

Your colours change as you change, and your colour choices may be different each time you do the SICA, especially the colours that reflect your moods and feelings. They can vary in a day, by a change of attitude, mood, because of a happening in your life, or they may remain the same if you're one of those very stable even-tempered individuals.

One of the surprises that you will receive from the results of Chart II of the SICA is a new insight into the inner you, and into your immediate needs. By realising what you're asking for in your life at the moment, you can become more objective with yourself. You will discover greater inner satisfaction. Most important, the results will help you in deciding what colours to wear and when, and will help teach you how to use the energy of the right colour to enhance yourself.

Are you ready to begin? Don't forget, one colour for each answer.

A. *How do you feel at this particular time?*
(Pretend that there is no language except the language of

23

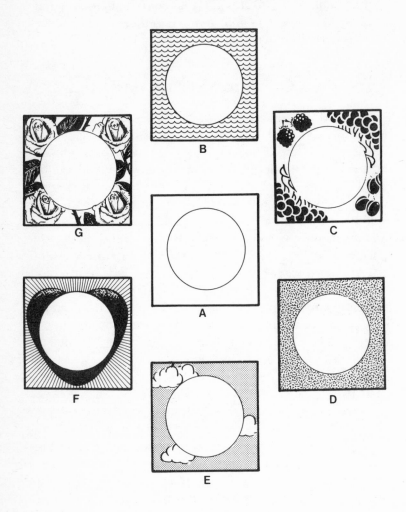

colour, and select a colour that identifies your feelings.)

B. *What colour do you associate with thirst?*
(Feel being very thirsty and quickly choose a colour that comes to mind.)

C. *When you think of something sweet, what colour comes to mind immediately?*
(You can associate anything with this sensing, but name its colour.)

D. *What colour corresponds to roughness as related to the sense of touch?*
(Select a colour that represents this tactile sensation to you.)

E. *What is your peaceful and calm colour?*
(Close your eyes and feel a colour that soothes and relaxes you.)

F. *What colour relates to the most recent powerful emotional experience that you've had?*
(Remember for a moment how you felt and choose a colour that identifies that feeling.)

G. *You have just heard some very exciting news! You feel great joy and happiness. What colour would you choose to express that feeling?*

You have now finished both parts of the self-portrait SICA, Chart I, your *communicative image*, and Chart II, the *intuitive, sensitive* you. There are no right or wrong answers, and you did not make any mistakes. After all, you are the artist who painted your image in the language of colour. It's now time to interpret how you see yourself. *Enjoy yourself!*

INTERPRETATION FOR YOUR SELF-PORTRAIT

Your answer to question No. 1 will show you your colour identity. The colour that you have selected will give you insight into that part of you that you acknowledge and communicate to others. Read it, and then move to the Creative Profiles to gain more insight into the meaning of the colour that you have chosen. This colour selection will identify some of your communicative strengths.

Colour 1	*The colour that you have chosen to represent you acknowledges your image strengths.*
	You see yourself as:
RED	Ambitious, energetic, courageous, extroverted
PINK	Affectionate, loving, compassionate, sympathetic
MAROON	Sensuous, emotional, gregarious, overly sensitive
ORANGE	Competent, action-oriented, organised, impatient
PEACH	Gentle, charitable, dexterous, enthusiastic
YELLOW	Communicative, expressive, social, people-oriented
MINT GREEN	Modest, insightful, composed, kind-hearted
APPLE GREEN	Innovative, adventurous, self-motivated, changeable
GREEN	Benevolent, humanistic, service-oriented, scientific

BLUE-GREEN (teal)	Idealistic, faithful, sentimental, inventive
LIGHT BLUE	Creative, perceptive, imaginative, analytical
DARK BLUE	Intelligent, executive, responsible, self-reliant
MAUVE	Delicate, reserved, sensitive, encouraging
PURPLE	Intuitive, feelingful, regal, spiritual
BROWN	Honest, down-to-earth, supportive, structured
BLACK	Disciplined, strong-willed, independent, opinionated
WHITE	Individualistic, egocentric, lonely, having low self-esteem
GREY	Passive, non-committal, stressed, over-burdened
SILVER	Honourable, chivalrous, trustworthy, romantic
GOLD	Idealistic, noble, successful, having high values

CREATIVE PROFILES

Below are listed creative profiles for each colour. Learning about your identity colours will help you become more aware of your self-image portrait. As with colours, there are many aspects to your palette. Be open to yourself and the personal colours of your rainbow.

RED

For your identity colour you have chosen the flashiest and most dramatic of all colours. Physical or emotional, 'very human' is another name for you. You can be dynamic and direct but also generous. You, red, have a strong character and love to be active and competitive. You are solid in knowing what you want, and usually win.

If a female, you have a tendency to react quickly and emotionally, not always objectively. As a male who chooses red, you like to be out in front, often in politics, for you enjoy accolades from others. Some people call you a gladiator, some call you a leader. As a leader, you have the ability and energy to move forward positively.

You are red, you are first, the Adam and Eve of society, the sexiest of all. You have strength, courage, and conviction of your rights, as well as wanting equal justice for all.

PINK

You have chosen the most loving, yet feminine of all colours. Your heart and your emotions are your strength. As a light pastel, you are soft and gentle. Your weakness surfaces only when you know not how to close your heart. Yet when hot pink is your identity colour, you become as strong as red. You may find your vulnerabilities in not recognising your emotionally draining friends.

'Mama or Papa of society' are your claims to fame. Responsibility for others is your game. Because you are a combination of red and white, you energise others as the nurturer and rescuer. Lover, sweetheart, and rose, you assert love, the universal symbol for caring and sharing. Receive as you give to bring balance to your big heart.

MAROON

Like a ruby, your identity colour is rich, rich red, the colour of the sensualist and the colour of the sensitive. Humour you have, for you enjoy fun and adventure, especially when the sun goes down. Your emotions are your strength. When positive, you always acquire positions of authority, but when emotionally upset, watch out, you can be volatile with anger or inflexibility.

You wear power naturally and easily. You have chosen the famed colour of Rome. Love of life, and bounties of pleasurable things, are your banner. Your restless heart heals with play, laughter, and song, for your emotions require much expression to flow. Entertain and be entertained, for all the world loves you! Aren't you the colour of burgundy?

ORANGE

Orange is a colour of form and design. Your energy is high, and as a warm colour, you are sometimes restless. Yet your competence and capabilities to organise are unmatched by any other colour. An architect or engineer, a designer or marketer – you'll find your niche in these professions. You are the great self-starter and motivator. To get the job done is your goal, for your energy always requires a direction.

You like form and structure around you because you are very conscious of design. No messy homes or offices for you, for they make you feel 'down'. You flow straight as an arrow when focused. Like the sun at dawn, you give purpose to all who know you! After all, aren't you the resource fuel of life, the colour of fire, the energy warmth for humankind?

PEACH

You have selected one of the most popular and social colours with which to identify. You're the colour of a delicious fruit or the sky at sunrise. Gentle as pink, but action-oriented as orange you can be. Yet you have your own identity, that of a gentle doer or humanitarian.

You have the power to secure or stimulate the emotions of others, as you love to be emotionally independent yourself and have the freedom to do as you please. You make the best colour for classrooms and dining-rooms, for children love you. Helping others to nourish and nurture themselves is your most attractive strength. Your only weakness is that you don't recognise your worth, as sometimes your pink or big heart gets in the way.

YELLOW

You have selected yellow, the colour of the universal communicator. You love your mouth. Sometimes you talk too much, but all the world listens to your sharing. At times you're happy, at times you're funny, you're always good in sales. When you learn to listen, many see you as the great counsellor, as you are sought for your talents to advise. The Egyptians and Mayans worshipped you, the colour of the sun, for your power to sustain life.

You are bright and expressive and give warmth to many. You're the life of the party, the best friend of man and the voice of the country. Be the shining light for others. Hold on to your personal energy, though; it can be wasted, especially when your questions run away with you.

MINT GREEN

Cooling to the body and emotions, you are like ice cream on a hot summer's day. You have chosen the most insightful of all colours as your identity, for you prefer to use your mental capabilities with your heart. You are green mixed with white, giving you the power of knowing what another is needy of, as well as aiding them to help themselves. 'Modesty' is another one of your virtuous descriptions, since you prefer the dynamic reds to be out in front, not you! You don't deal well with strong emotional outbursts or loud 'anythings', as you prefer to be left quietly alone to pursue your goals.

You'll be found in many alternative healing professions or just seeking knowledge to enhance your life. The aesthetic harmonies of philosophy and natural arts appeal to you in a very special way. If one is to look, one will always discover you graciously serving without fanfare, hoping to make the world a little better.

APPLE GREEN

You have selected for your identity the colour of spring grass, or a delicious green apple. A combination of pale yellow and green, you are extremely flexible and everyone's friend. People like you because of your open mind and adventurous spirit. You are usually found creating a new project or enterprise where you can quickly rise to the top. But there you won't stay, for you become too easily bored with anything routine.

Changeable, adventurous, and exciting you are, but not always sensitive to your own emotional needs. You like your mind to be stimulated rather than your heart, so you can go, go, go to the top. Your greatest asset is your outgoing interest in everything, from the stars to the rocks. Most of all, you like to enhance and expand yourself, to become everything you are.

GREEN

As a green identity, you have the strongest interest in the healing arts. You usually are found serving and aiding others in humanistic ways. Your compassion always surrounds the wanting, as well as those who are less fortunate than you. You have good perception and awareness about most things, but you don't appreciate sudden surprises. You're too stable to have your boat unexpectedly rocked.

When your shade is darker green, you love to be recognised

31

for your superior mind, which enjoys details and balanced ledger sheets. Some call you a healer, yet some may call you a scientist. As a practitioner, your skills are unequalled, for you can usually see clearly into any situation. Health and balance are your goals, for you would like to discover life's hidden secrets, as well as return the earth and all its habitants to natural harmony.

BLUE-GREEN (teal)

The colour of the ocean, of trees wet with rain, or the coolness of sparkling brooks – you flow with movement and self-contained energy. If you have chosen blue-green (teal) for identity, others find you hopeful, optimistic, believing, and trusting. You have more than enough of faith and hope, for you easily trust yourself and others. Professionally you'll be found in the helping arts of the mind or spirit, and often standing behind a podium.

Your contemporary acceptance in today's colour world enables you as a royalty hue to give faith to others. Not green, the healer, not blue, the intellectual, but a combination of the qualities of both, you are! Some seek you for enlightenment, others for practical insight; for whoever seeks you, you offer inner calmness. Faith is your middle name.

LIGHT BLUE

You, the colour of the sky at midday, are the most artistic and creative of all the colours. Imagination is your name. You love your mind and strive to express it freely. Sometimes it's hard to relax; you want to reach for the stars to bring them into form. Art, music, and literature stimulate you. When motivated to solve a problem, you have a strong creative sense of insight, as well as praticality. These traits permit you to enjoy a position among the great minds of society.

32

From the art world to the marketplace you'll be found, creating ideas, pictures, and form, always bringing in the new. You like to design businesses that serve the needs of the public, as well as creatively invest in new ventures. The universe has blessed you with its spark of imagination, so go for it, express it all the way!

DARK BLUE

You have chosen the colour that identifies as the wisest of colours. You could be a judge, executive, or business manager, for you enjoy decision-making. Being very wise, you show good judgement of character. People respect you for your intellect. You are the favourite suit of lawmakers.

As a female, you have a tendency to be too independent and a little bossy. As a male, you see yourself so self-managed that sometimes it's difficult to accept advice from others. Yet you both are the universal teachers, for you love your knowledge and its authority.

Some people call you the boss, some call you the head. But as the head, you are not always aware of the needs of your body. You are the person who knows who you are and where you are going. Your balance is your heart, so stay in touch with your feelings. They will guide you to the needs of yourself, as well as to the sensitivity of others.

MAUVE

If you have chosen this calm, gentle colour, mauve, for your identity, you are sensitive, delicate, reserved, yet nurturing to others. You have become the rage of the workplace; all women like what you represent – their supportive friend. Men are not quite used to you as yet, for you magnify their gentleness and intuitive nature.

As a male who identifies with the colour mauve, you like to be known for your sensitivities. But you may need to seek a little more blue in your rainbow, for you are not always objective with your emotions and heart.

Some people call you the flower of the earth, or the violet rose of a sunset. As a colour you have the ability to give peace to all. You are mauve, the new feelingful colour of humanity, the most sensitive of all.

PURPLE

Purple or violet is the most intuitive of all colours. Like the amethyst, you are spiritual and thoughtful. Intuition is your name, for you are very gifted. Sometimes you're shy and hiding like the violet, other times noble and regal as the ruler. But always, you have high values for yourself and others. You prefer to look up rather than down. Because of your sensitivity, you have difficulty in trusting others completely.

Some call you spiritual, others call you religious. Whatever you are called, your faith will always see you through. You have the gift of feeling; not only for yourself, but you can help others to find their way. Always listen to yourself, for you are truly a gem of grace.

BROWN

You have identified as brown, the colour of the earth. You are supportive and stable like a rock. Others see you as secure, some call you strength; you exhibit 'lean upon me' properties. You always bring everything into order, for you have the gift of inner security. Honesty is your high virtue, as you have no time for exaggeration and frills. Your only vulnerability appears when you can't express yourself. You like to be heard.

Similar to the farmer and earth guardian, you find your professions close to nature. You like working with your hands. Secure, supportive, and dexterous, you belong to the country, for you are the machine that helps it grow – and the protector of the earth.

BLACK

If you have identified as the colour black, you appear disciplined and protective of yourself. Black is powerful, black is mighty, but black can also be closed to light and openness. Sometimes black can be used for strength, sometimes for protection, but black can image a barrier between you and others. You may desire not to share but to stay locked alone in your world. Yet, you can be the favourite outfit to go any place or can mix and match with any colour. You give a strong, authoritative image of yourself.

But if you've chosen black because of being despondent or down, open the door and let the sunshine in. Call a friend or call for help. You might just find a rainbow waiting with a pot of love and rewards.

WHITE

White is another achromatic that seeks to find other colours of the rainbow. When you choose it as your identity colour, you probably are going through a transition. White is universal and abstract, a new idea without form. You are the ego, the individual, the wanderer, but for ever alone. You have selected a simplistic and pure colour, but one that reaches out for recognition.

Combined with the colour red, mixed with blue, or as an additive to any colour, you will change your hue. You search for your own truth; don't escape into your own abstraction. Come out to play. Join with others to make a colourful array. Some may call you a loner, but don't be alone, for you really desire a family and identity to belong to.

GREY

You have chosen a neutral, named the famous monochromatic or achromatic. For superb contrast to any colour, you are unequalled. Yet grey has little energy of its own because of its total passivity. You may feel tired, fatigued, or stressed today, for your energy is low. When you flow, all the rainbow colours belong to you as you set them to shine.

Play is your goal, and a vacation should be in the offing. With laughter you'll find more sensitivity to your needs, as you rest and revitalise. Some now find you low, some will see you tired, so pick up your colour with the sun and sea. Don't be grey; be carefree!

SILVER

You have chosen a colour of one of the precious metals, silver. Your sense of self-worth is high. Like the knights and ladies of old, you come to the rescue of others. You are romantic, for you always find the best in everyone, rich or poor alike. As a shield you like to protect others. But when you lose sight of your own worth, your shine loses its lustre.

As a setting for most other colours, you make the best of friends. Your trustworthiness is unsurpassed. Others must earn your trust, though, for you have difficulty once it is broken. Rather than extending yourself out to the public, you prefer the limelight to come to you. Advocate and attorney fits your mould, for your 'metal' can always be tested. You are the colour of honour.

GOLD

Gold is the hue of wealth. You have a very rich nature, and in turn you make a strong securer for all people. In spirit, you as gold are the highest ideal and virtue. You enjoy shooting for the stars and settle for nothing less. You like grandeur, extravagance, and plenty. But your undoing can be your dreams, for when they are shattered or broken, you turn inward and attack yourself.

You are the best, you are the greatest, you're always worth

your weight. Some may see you as fantastic, others see you as high-minded and proud. When melted, your strength extends to leadership or to support, for you are the awareness of the top and the dream for the future. You secure everyone.

INTERPRETATION FOR COLOUR NO. 2

Continue to interpret your answers for colour No. 2, in order to learn more about your image. Your colour choice here will show you where you find your source of inspiration. This colour is your pick-me-up colour! It always looks good with your identity colour.

Colour 2	*The colour you have chosen for inspiration helps you get in touch with what you need to inspire yourself and to give a good image of yourself.*
	You feel good when you:
RED	Get physical exercise, achieve or pursue ambitious goals, compete
PINK	Accept yourself, give and receive love, nurture others
MAROON	Have fun, and are adventurous and sensual
ORANGE	Organise goals, use energy constructively, are focused and productive
PEACH	Express and nurture yourself, demand equal opportunity
YELLOW	Socialise, communicate, and express yourself to others
MINT GREEN	Are objective, in control of your emotions, and see clearly

APPLE GREEN	Change, begin new projects, and are challenged
GREEN	Serve and help others, develop yourself, and see things clearly
BLUE-GREEN (teal)	Are truthful to yourself, follow your ideals, and are optimistic
LIGHT BLUE	Use your imagination, express yourself artistically, have creative outlets, and are practical
DARK BLUE	Manage yourself, are independent and self-reliant
MAUVE	Listen to your instincts, believe in yourself, and follow your inner guidance
PURPLE	Trust your feelings, use your intuition, are recognised as sensitive
BROWN	Are self-confident, secure, aware of your self-worth
BLACK	Are disciplined, independent, self-sufficient, meeting your own standards
WHITE	Have new ideas, creative insights, and an unregimented lifestyle
GREY	Rest from stress, relax, remain uninvolved
SILVER	Seek truth, are honest, and recognise your own worth
GOLD	Pursue high ideals and goals, and reap and accept their rewards

INTERPRETATION FOR COLOUR NO. 3

Read and interpret your colour responses for question No. 3. This colour aids you in understanding how your best image is extended. It is a positive, securing colour, for it will show what helps to balance you. Not only a key to better communication with your image, but one that continually helps you to stay in touch with yourself. This colour should always be in your wardrobe, so you can use it as a colour for balancing yourself.

Colour 3	*The colour you have chosen guides you to a better understanding of yourself.*
	You bring yourself into balance with:
RED	Physical accomplishments, leadership roles, positive progress, success and triumphs
PINK	Love, self-nurturing, emotional support from others, and being nice to self
MAROON	Sensual pleasures, emotional expression, music, dance, and dinner out once a week
ORANGE	Organisation, productive use of time and energy, successful completion of goals
PEACH	Social activities, pursuit of community service, and active participation in charitable organisations
YELLOW	Self-expression, sharing yourself, and an optimistic attitude and smile
MINT GREEN	Continual self-development classes, involvements in New Age projects, and following beauty and health regimes
APPLE GREEN	New interests, challenges, self-regeneration, and playing of games of chance

GREEN	Self-awareness development, self-improvement, and health and science pursuits
BLUE-GREEN (teal)	Artistic self-expression, involvement in church or spiritual groups, and quiet, creative play
LIGHT BLUE	Creativity, imagination, self-expression, use of knowledge for problem solving
DARK BLUE	Self-management, self-reliance, independence, and responsibility for others
MAUVE	Sensitive support from others, reliance on instinctive feeling, and time for meditation or relaxation
PURPLE	Trust in, and honouring of, your intuitive inner feelings, and more time for listening
BROWN	Energy from the earth and natural elements, acquired personal security and self-worth
BLACK	Discipline, self-imposed guidelines, total self-reliance, and opportunities for independence
WHITE	New ideas, creative insights, a simplified lifestyle, and more time for self
GREY	Rest, relaxation, lessening of involvements and stress, and a planned vacation
SILVER	A sense of self-worth, higher self-esteem, self-enhancement, and more trust of others
GOLD	Satisfaction from sucessful accomplishments and/or high attainments and goals

INTERPRETATION FOR COLOUR NO. 4

Your answers for this part of your self-portrait will show you how you recognise yourself in others. You can see how your friends and associates extend your talents and strengths. Like the old proverb 'One is known by the company they keep', the colour that you have chosen expresses another rainbow part of you!

Colour 4   *The colour you have chosen for harmony helps you recognise more of your strengths, those attributes you like to see in others.*

Your best friends and associates can be:

RED   Positive people, leaders, politicians, or industrialists

PINK   Rescuers, nurturers, humanitarian benefactors, or childlike persons

MAROON   Fun-lovers, comedians, risk-takers, or sensualists

ORANGE   Architects, builders, market designers, or engineers

PEACH   Humanitarians, club or organisation elected officials, or community leaders

YELLOW   Salespeople, consultants, counsellors, or public arbitrators

MINT GREEN   Natural healers, health food enthusiasts, poets, or beauty counsellors

APPLE GREEN   Innovators, freethinkers, initiators, or adventurers

GREEN   Healers, therapists, humanists, or scientists

BLUE-GREEN (teal)	Futurists, missionaries, behavioural scientists, or spiritual mentors
LIGHT BLUE	Artists, designers, planners, or analysts
DARK BLUE	Executives, professionals, educators, or philosophers
MAUVE	Interior decorators, intuitive or sensitive artists, or spiritual counsellors
PURPLE	Theologians, spiritual leaders, ministers, or philosophers
BROWN	Skilled workers, machine operators, farmers, or lovers of the earth
BLACK	Disciplinarians, authorities, dictators, or protectors
WHITE	Individualists, loners, or egocentric or lonely people
GREY	Non-committal associates, pacifists, uninvolved peers, or quiet people
SILVER	Crusaders, honourable friends, lawyers, or champions of justice
GOLD	High achievers or successful people, financiers, or futurists

INTERPRETATION FOR COLOUR NO. 5

This is a fun interpretation as your colour answer for this question will identify who makes the best partner for you. Many relationships change as we evolve, and often we're not sure exactly what colour (type of person) we partner with the best. The colour that you have chosen identifies 'Mr' or 'Ms

Right' for now! But remember, you're the artist, and as you change, your choice might change.

Colour 5	*The colour that you have chosen for contrast and support helps you recognise your most compatible partnership.*

If you are a woman, the man who makes the best partner for you is:

RED	A down-to-earth, sensuous lover
PINK	A father-type, or childlike sweetheart love
MAROON	A self-indulgent but fun-loving lover
ORANGE	An organiser and builder, motivator and work partner
PEACH	A kind and gentle man who cares
YELLOW	A buddy, friend, or mentor partner
MINT GREEN	A therapist, or practitioner in the health arts
APPLE GREEN	A new partner, or a change in partnership
GREEN	A medical or humanitarian partner
BLUE-GREEN (teal)	An independent but mentally stimulating partner
LIGHT BLUE	An artist or creative partner
DARK BLUE	A business or executive partner
MAUVE	A partner sensitive to your feelings
PURPLE	A minister or spiritual partner
BROWN	A steady, supportive, secured partner
BLACK	No partnership because of over self-reliance
WHITE	An individual who is a loner

GREY	A submissive man who supports you
SILVER	A knight in shining armour
GOLD	A banker or wealthy man

If you are a man, the woman who makes the best partner for you is:

RED	A vivacious, sensuous woman
PINK	A mother- or daughter-type sweetheart
MAROON	A fun-loving, non-serious woman
ORANGE	A self-motivated, independent woman
PEACH	A compassionate, community-oriented woman
YELLOW	A social and communicative woman
MINT GREEN	An idealistic and comforting woman
APPLE GREEN	A challenge, or a new woman
GREEN	A health-conscious or healer partner
BLUE-GREEN (teal)	A mentally inspiring partner
LIGHT BLUE	An artist or creative partner
DARK BLUE	A businesswoman or equal partner
MAUVE	An intuitive spiritual partner
PURPLE	A sensitive and noble woman
BROWN	A steady, supportive, subservient partner
BLACK	No partnership because of over-abundance of self-reliance
WHITE	An unattached, lonely woman

SILVER   A romantic, trustworthy friend

GOLD   A self-accomplished, successful woman

INTERPRETATION FOR COLOUR NO. 6

Have you ever wondered why or for what reason you might not give a good first impression, or what your weak points are? Your dislike colours can aid you to find out. Your 'yuk' colour will reveal to you those hidden weaknesses or areas of your image that need more improvement. Your colour choice for a dislike colour will give clues in determining your vulner-abilities.

Colour 6   *The colour that you have chosen for your yuk colour helps you recognise your major vulnerabilities.*

Your weakness shows up when you place yourself in situations where you:

RED (such as: rose reds, fire-engine red, or magenta reds)   Can't control your temper or emotional outbursts and become angry with yourself

PINK (such as: rose pink, carnation pink, or hot pink)   Feel dependent on others, or feel over-burdened by outside dependencies

MAROON (such as: deep reds, or brick reds)   Feel victimised or resentful because of the actions of others

ORANGE (such as: bright orange or burnt orange)   Feel confused, frustrated, or blocked

PEACH (such as: apricot and salmon)   Feel disorganised with your time and energy or are embarrassed because of it

YELLOW (such as: banana, intense yellow, or mustard yellow)   Feel you are not living up to your own expectations, or are threatened by others' criticism

MINT GREEN (such as: pale green or aqua)   Feel unhappy with yourself because of lack of emotional stimulation or challenge

APPLE GREEN (Yellow-greens, such as: chartreuse, avocado, or khaki green)   Feel that you can't express yourself or your opinions

GREEN (such as: grass, medium green, or pine green)   Feel bored or stymied because of lack of self-motivation or opportunity

BLUE-GREEN (teal) (such as: turquoise or peacock blue-green)   Feel emotional stress due to loss of faith or hope in yourself and others

BLUES(any blue: light, medium, or dark blue)   Feel mentally stressed due to lack of play and relaxation

MAUVE (such as: lavender or rose beige)   Feel that others restrict or are insensitive to your feelings

PURPLE (such as: orchid, violet, or grape) — Feel imposed upon by others' belief systems, religions, regulations, or rules

BROWN (such as: tan, beige, or dark browns) — Feel consumed by worry or permit fear or guilt to control you

BLACK — Feel despondent or depressed because of lack of self-recognition and insufficent love of self

WHITE — Feel lonely, unloved, separated emotionally, or detached.

GREY — Feel rejection, or fear, or failure due to lack of self-acceptance or self-respect

SILVER — Feel dishonoured by broken trusts

GOLD — Feel the loss of success or financial rewards

INTERPRETATION FOR COLOUR NO. 7

The colour that you have chosen for No. 7 is a very important colour, as it's the colour that makes the best impression for a positive communicative image. In fact, it is your most personal communicative colour! You might find that it can help you put your 'best foot forward', expanding your image and working at the same time to motivate you. When translated from the colour language to verbal language, you'll discover what your important motivation stimulants are.

Colour 7 — *The colour that you have chosen for your motivation colour helps you to expand your image and stimulate a positive impression of yourself!*

Your strongest motivating factors are:

RED — Your personal recognition, power, positive attitude concerning your completion of goals

PINK — Loving relationships, responsibility for caring for others, and emotional fulfilments

MAROON — Emotional reinforcement, fun, adventure, emotional and physical play

ORANGE — Organisation, goal planning, designing and building of projects, self-accomplishments

PEACH — Participation in humanitarian ventures and projects, being charitable, and acceptance of community-action roles

YELLOW — Socialising, expressing self, counselling, advising, and sharing in group activities

MINT GREEN — Self-awareness, self-health, and serving others in a humanistic manner

APPLE GREEN — New interests, change of old habits, new opportunities and challenges

GREEN — Clear insight, self-recognition, independence, and freedom of practice and action

BLUE-GREEN (teal) — Any enhancement practices for self-growth, freedom for choices, and better living opportunities

LIGHT BLUE — Creative or artistic projects or hobbies, problems to solve, mental games to play

DARK BLUE — Insights of wisdom, self-responsibility, knowledge, and management role-playing

MAUVE   Recognition of, sensitivity to, and trust of, personal intuitive and instinctual feelings

PURPLE   Teaching and preaching spiritual values, regal self-acceptance and assuredness

BROWN   Emotional and physical security, self-worth and self-trust, freedom from worry

BLACK   Total independence of action, self-sufficiency, authoritative positions

WHITE   New ideas to act upon, a more simplified lifestyle, freedom from outside pressures

GREY   Relaxation, more free time, less involvements in daily stresses, and rest

SILVER   Practices of self-worth, honesty, trust of friends, and the value of truth

GOLD   High ideals, self-satisfaction in success, aspirations of high goals.

Identity, inspiration, balance, vulnerability, motivation or even partnership – all these parts of your image can be recognised by translating the language of colour into words. Your self-portrait may differ from what you think you are, but take some time just visualising it. You might see new talents, as you the artist have imaged it, so enjoy interpreting SICA, the game of the language of colour. Your reward will be positive communicative strengths to work upon!

CHART II

You are now ready to interpret the second part of your SICA, Chart II. These interpretations will help show you how in touch you are with yourself through feeling and sensing. They will give you insight about the intuitive you. Your colour choices will offer 'colour response meanings' for personal interpretations of your feelings and your sensing abilities. They'll show inner communication between you, the designer of your image, and you, the intuitive artist.

To begin, you'll want to know how you were feeling when you answered the SICA questions. So, we'll start with colour A. Your colour response will express similar to verbal language your mood or attitude at the time you were choosing or colouring your circles. Your colour answer for A will not necessarily tell you how you were feeling yesterday or the day before, only *now*, when doing the SICA. Remember your colours change as you change, and your response may be different tomorrow, but it will help you see yourself today! Enjoy!

INTERPRETATIONS FOR COLOUR A

How are you feeling at this particular time – an interesting question and answer for you. Your colour choice will set the mood for your intuitive self-portrait of yourself. Like the artist, you've chosen the hue or tone for your painting! You'll recognise where you're coming from, or how you're respond-ing to your own feelings. Read on to discover how you're intuitively feeling!

Colour A	*The colour that you have chosen for how you're feeling helps you to see the tone of your inner self-portrait.*
	At the time you chose the colour for how you were feeling, you were responding to yourself:
RED	........................Emotionally

PINK	......................Lovingly
MAROON	......................Moodily
ORANGE	......................With some confusion
PEACH	......................Approvingly
YELLOW	......................Openly
MINT GREEN	......................Calmly
APPLE-GREEN	......................Adventurously
GREEN	......................With some boredom
BLUE-GREEN (teal)	......................Mechanically
LIGHT BLUE	......................Analytically
DARK BLUE	......................With some mental exhaustion
MAUVE	......................Intuitively
PURPLE	......................Over-sensitively
BROWN	......................With some uncertainty
BLACK	......................With some despair
WHITE	......................With some loneliness
GREY	......................With some emotional fatigue
SILVER	......................With new self-respect
GOLD	......................Materially

INTERPRETATION FOR COLOUR B

Your answer for this part of your self-portrait will show you what you can use to expand your happiness and self-satisfaction. By associating a colour with an unsatiated feeling or desire, you'll see how it offers you a happy solution.

Colour B   *The colour that you have chosen for thirst helps you recognise an inner desire, one that you would like to satisfy.*

My feelings tell me that I need more:

RED
Physical exercise and emotional expression
(Maybe a love affair or romantic interlude?
If not, an exercise regime is a must!)

PINK
Acceptance and love of myself
(Maybe a special treat for me today,
tomorrow, and every week from now on?)

MAROON
Emotional relaxation and recharging
(Maybe a little play, song, and dance?)

ORANGE
Self-accomplishment and recognition of my
goals
(Maybe less frustration and more positive
focusing on my career development?)

PEACH
Involvement in humanitarian projects or
organisations
(Maybe accept a leadership role in the
school or community?)

YELLOW
Sharing of my personal thoughts and
feelings to make room for laughter
(Maybe a good friend or counsellor to talk
to?)

MINT GREEN
Awareness of my image, my body, and the
power of my mind
(Maybe a self-development or self-
enhancement class?)

APPLE-GREEN | Challenge in my work or play
(Maybe a new job or new relationship)

GREEN | Health consciousness and attention to my personal needs
(Maybe a new plan for work, play, rest, and eating properly?)

BLUE-GREEN (teal) | Optimism and renewal of my faith and hope
(Maybe an affirmation or prayer each day to recognise daily gifts?)

LIGHT BLUE | Artistic or creative hobbies for my self-expression
(Maybe a little more insight into my creative powers through any art form?)

DARK BLUE | Self-responsibility and reliance upon my own judgement
(Maybe *I* should become the decision-maker?)

MAUVE | Recognition of my own intuitive powers and instinctual abilities
(Maybe I should pay more attention to my feelings?)

PURPLE | Sensitivity to my personal and spiritual needs
(Maybe I should try yoga or meditation to release my mind blocks?)

BROWN | Confidence and inner security, and less worry in my life
(Maybe I should work on trust and self-confidence in myself?)

BLACK | Self-imposed guidelines and disciplines
(Maybe a little more restriction on my wasting of time and energy?)

WHITE	Insight, perception, and greater awareness into myself and my life (Maybe a little more openness to myself and to new ways of living?)
GREY	Rest, relaxation, and freedom from daily stress (Maybe I am due a vacation, sun and sea?)
SILVER	Self-worth, respect, and self-esteem (Maybe I should accept myself more as I honour others?)
GOLD	Self-satisfaction from recognition of my dreams and high goals (Maybe my goals are within reach?)

INTERPRETATION FOR COLOUR C

Your answer for this part of your intuitive self-portrait will guide you to a better understanding of how accurate your sensual perception can be. Sweet sensations are pleasing to us; in fact, some of us tend to be 'sweet freaks' as often we crave a sweet fix to satisfy any desire. Through the language of colour you'll explore what 'colour meanings' are associated with sweet and pleasing to the senses at the same time. You'll have fun discovering how well your inner communication system works – a sense and a colour working together. You may even discern that one of your important senses may tell it all!

Colour C	*The colour that you have chosen will help you to identify what you find pleasing and satisfying through sensing.*
	How sweet it is to:
RED	Be physically satisfied

PINK	Be lovingly satisfied
MAROON	Be emotionally satisfied
ORANGE	Have my appetites satisfied
PEACH	Be satisfied with myself
YELLOW	Be open to all my sensing
MINT GREEN	Be quiet and calm within
APPLE GREEN	Be able to self-express
GREEN	Have good balance and health
BLUE-GREEN (teal)	Be spiritually satisfied
LIGHT BLUE	Be creatively satisfied
DARK BLUE	Be intellectually satisfied
MAUVE	Accept my intuitive feelings
PURPLE	Be recognised for my sensitivity
BROWN	Be emotionally secure and accepted by others
BLACK	Be closed to my sensing
WHITE	Be separated from reality
GREY	Be out of touch with my sensing
SILVER	Be out of touch with my sensing
GOLD	Be out of touch with my sensing

INTERPRETATION FOR COLOUR D

Colour D is your last colour choice associating a colour with sensing. The rest of the colour interpretations will concern colour for feeling and attitudes. But this colour for roughness corresponds to your sense of touch and the tactile sensation that the colour evokes. You'll once again recognise that you, colour, and your sensing can communicate intuitively.

Colour D	*The colour that you have chosen for roughness helps you to recognise what energy you do not find soothing to your senses. You may consider it the colour of an internal stress.*

You respond uncomfortably to:

RED	......................Uncontrolled anger
PINK	......................Over-emotional dependency
MAROON	......................Emotional victimisation
ORANGE	......................Discord and confusion
PEACH	......................Embarrassment or disgrace
YELLOW	......................Unwarranted criticism
MINT GREEN	......................Complacency or inactivity
APPLE GREEN	......................Emotional repression
GREEN	......................Loss of personal freedom
BLUE-GREEN (teal)	......................Personal disillusionment
LIGHT BLUE	......................Unsolved problems
DARK BLUE	......................Mental exhaustion
MAUVE	......................Insensitivity of others
PURPLE	......................Restriction by authority
BROWN	......................Excessive worry or guilt

56

BLACK	......................Despair or depression
WHITE	......................Loneliness or isolation
GREY	......................Rejection or failure
SILVER	......................Dishonesty or deception
GOLD	......................Loss of material welfare

INTERPRETATION FOR COLOUR E

Continue interpreting your colour answers for your self-portrait. Your colour choice will show you how well you and your feelings communicate, and when you're most in touch with your inner strength and peace.

Colour E   *The colour that you have chosen for calm helps you recognise inner strengths. These powers are an endless source of supply for you.*

You feel strong and emotionally secure when you are:

RED	Positive, energetic, and emotionally expressive
PINK	Loving, compassionate, and empathetic
MAROON	Kind, hospitable, and accepting your sensuality
ORANGE	Motivated, focused, and organised
PEACH	Charitable to yourself and others
YELLOW	Sharing, communicating, and expressing yourself
MINT GREEN	Composed, at peace with yourself and the world

APPLE GREEN	Innovative, challenged, happy, and healthy
GREEN	Serving and helping others with insight and understanding
BLUE-GREEN (teal)	Believing in yourself and faith in others
LIGHT BLUE	Creative, practical, and using your mind instead of your heart
DARK BLUE	In charge of and responsible for self and others
MAUVE	Listening to your intuitive and instinctual feelings
PURPLE	Aware of your sensitivities and believe in your own inner guidance
BROWN	Self-confident, self-secure, and understanding of your self-worth
BLACK	Self-disciplined and following your own directives and guidelines
WHITE	Open-minded, clear, and ready for new insights and new ideas
GREY	Relaxed, rested, and emotionally uninvolved
SILVER	Trusting and accepting of others, and being truthful to yourself
GOLD	Satisfied, successful, and working towards your goals

INTERPRETATION FOR COLOUR F

The colour that you have chosen for F helps you to see, because of the language of colour, your reaction to strong emotional stimuli. You permit this energy feeling to express a most intense part of you.

Colour F	*This colour will indicate your positive or not-so-positive emotional response to a powerful experience. Look and see both meanings of this colour. They might just shed a litle more light onto your 'feeling' and 'sensing' energy makeup.*

You react strongly to:

	Positive	*Not so positive*
RED	Physical/emotional love	Anger
PINK	Caring love	Over-burdening
MAROON	Self-loving	Victimisation
ORANGE	Satisfaction of my needs (such as food)	Frustration
PEACH	Championing for right	Embarrassment
YELLOW	Sharing	Criticism
MINT GREEN	Self-enhancing	Inactivity
APPLE GREEN	Innovating	Repression
GREEN	Physical health needs	Boredom
BLUE-GREEN (teal)	Higher faith	Patronising
LIGHT BLUE	Mind expansion	Mental exhaustion
DARK BLUE	Decision-making	Nervousness
MAUVE	Channelling	Lack of freedom

PURPLE	Social acceptance	Invasion of personal privacy
BROWN	Personal security	Guilt
BLACK	Self-power	Depression
WHITE	Little reaction	Separation
GREY	No reaction	Fatigue
SILVER	Honour and ideals	Unworthiness
GOLD	Material possessions	Loss

INTERPRETATION FOR COLOUR G

This is the happiest colour choice of all! Why? Because it is the colour that you have chosen for something wonderful. Your colour expresses an inner joy that you feel. When you feel elevated and stimulated, you express this colour and send clear signals from your feelings to your mind, expanding the image of yourself.

Colour G *The colour that you have chosen for joy and happiness helps you recognise the happy, communicative you!*

You feel the happiest when you are:

RED Positive in thought, in action, and in accomplishment

PINK Loving yourself and accepting love as you love others

MAROON Emotionally relaxed, secure, and having fun

ORANGE Self-motivated, organised, and focused on your goals

PEACH	Sharing love and commitment in humanitarian programmes
YELLOW	Expressing yourself, communicating, and sharing with others
MINT GREEN	Expanding and gaining insight into your own self-awareness
APPLE GREEN	Beginning new projects, adventures, and opportunities that challenge
GREEN	Helping and serving others to restore their balance
BLUE-GREEN (teal)	Following, acting on, and practising your personal beliefs
LIGHT BLUE	Activating your creative mind as a designer or problem-solver
DARK BLUE	Taking responsibility to manage and educate others
MAUVE	Using your intuitive insights as a resource for aiding others
PURPLE	Trusting and recognising your sensitivities as gems of great value
BROWN	Secure within yourself concerning your inherent talents to provide self-survival
BLACK	Have control of yourself in order to communicate an authoritative image
WHITE	Open to new ideas and new perceptions concerning yourself and projects
GREY	Relaxed, released from over-involvements, and have freedom from stress

SILVER   Truthful to yourself, and believing in your
                self-worth and valour

GOLD   Stimulated by obtaining personal goals,
                success and acquisitions of wealth

You have now finished both parts of the SICA, Chart I and Chart II – your self-portrait through the language of colour. For Chart I, you have used your creative imaging to see yourself and to recognise your strong communicative strengths. In Chart II, you used your sensing and feeling about colour to give you insight into the intuitive you. You might want to write down the verbal responses to your colour selections in order to see your entire self-portrait – how you think you see yourself and how you feel about you.

In the next chapters you'll learn how to make your SICA portrait work for you, not just by analysing your image, but by recognising how you can put your SICA results to practical use. Try it in planning a communicative wardrobe, for a better image of yourself and for greater productivity.

3

*How to Use the SICA
to Improve Your Life*

SICA portraits can only be inspirational if you choose to act upon your own unique qualities. The SICA discloses your talents, but you supply the action.

Your self-portrait can guide you artistically to a better understanding of yourself. It offers means for greater insight, inspiration, and motivation. Below are some guidelines to help you further interpret your SICA.

After you have matched the verbal responses to your selected colours from Charts I and II of your self-portrait, sit back and take a few minutes to get acquainted with the colours that you've chosen.

Guideline No. 1 Look and see how many times you have repeated the same colour in both charts – once, more than once, or many times.

Where, in what position, or with what number choice do you repeat the same colour?

Read again the 'colour response meanings' for the colour you've repeatedly used. This colour should tell you something about yourself, a strong message from you to you!

YOUR SELF-PORTRAIT

Chart I		Chart II	
Colour	◯ 1	Colour	◯ A
Colour	◯ 2	Colour	◯ B
Colour	◯ 3	Colour	◯ C
Colour	◯ 4	Colour	◯ D
Colour	◯ 5	Colour	◯ E
Colour	◯ 6	Colour	◯ F
Colour	◯ 7	Colour	◯ G

Remember, you have intuitively chosen your colours, so your self-portrait is an individual grouping of your colours, not necessarily those of your friends, workmates, or members of your family. They belong personally to you!

Guideline No. 2   Review Chart I, your creative image of yourself, and look at the colours that you have selected for inspiration (colour No. 2), balance (colour No. 3), and motivation (colour No. 7). These are all positive extensions of your image, as they make you look and feel good. When experiencing any of these 'colour response meanings' you are communicating well and expanding your positivity.

The colours that you have chosen for inspiration, balance, and motivation will not tell you what job you should be in, but they will give you insight into what you like to do and feel good doing!

In the next chapter, Colours for You, we'll explore further how and when to wear these colours. But for now, familiarise yourself with your positive strength colours, those that you have chosen to extend your image.

Guideline No. 3   Remembering the colour that you've chosen for 'yuk', and situations where you may need some improvement, permits you to take a look at one of your vulnerabilities. This personal colour certainly doesn't make you feel good, and you should not wear it or have it in your environment. Since there are other in-depth interpretations for 'yuk', do not focus a great deal on it. Rather, let the positive colours of your creative image be your game plan.

Guideline No. 4   The colour selections for Chart II help show you how in touch you are with yourself through feeling and sensing. They will give you insight about the 'intuitive you'. You will discover by your colour choices what you might need to bring greater happiness into your life.

First, the colour that you have selected for how you're feeling indicates your general mood or attitude. Look up again the colour meaning for how you're responding to yourself (colour A). The colour should not need further interpretation, for all you have to do is to look to colour B for your attitude colour change. By sensing, you have intuitively informed yourself of what you need at this moment in time, your answer from colour B. Your colour response for colour B offers you a happy solution for your current unmet need.

Guideline No. 5   You might ask how you determine what colour indicates problems that you are having difficulty dealing with. Once again, by asking your sensing intuitive ability, you can discover what stress you find difficult to handle. Your colour response for circle D can help your discovery. The colour that you have selected aids you in recognising your non-communicative internal stresses.

In order to manage the stress, look quickly to colour E for your answer. You are most in touch with your inner power with this colour choice. Read the meaning again and again, or say a positive affirmation: 'I feel strong and emotionally secure when I am_____'.

Guideline No. 6   The last colour choice, colour G, for your self-portrait is one of the most important of all. It helps you recognise the happy, communicative you, within yourself, between your feelings and your mind, and on the outside, between you and the world. This colour can be used anywhere, anytime, or any place. Your 'colour meaning' expresses what makes you the all-together, happy you.

After analysing your self-portrait, you might still want to see how others have used the SICA for their benefit. In the next few pages I have included a few stories on how the SICA has worked for others. You might compare their colour choices, the colour responses, and how they were aided by the SICA. All names have been changed, but the stories are true.

A HOUSEWIFE TURNED CREATIVELY PRODUCTIVE

I met Patricia, a homemaker, after a friend suggested that she have a SICA in an attempt to prevent further hospitalisation. In fact, her friend paid for this first SICA and even delivered it to the hospital for her to complete.

Two weeks went by and a beautiful woman appeared in my office wanting to change herself, her attitudes, her image, and her general lifestyle. The report on the SICA had imaged her as 'creative' (light blue) and her source of inspiration, colour 2 (yellow), 'communicative'. Unfortunately, in her present home life these qualities were not being expressed. Her 'yuk' colour, circle 6, was yellow-green, which indicated she had no outlets for self-expression. She was having difficulty in finding a real purpose for living. She had lost sight of who she was. During the next year, after completing four SICAs and a month's guidance under a counsellor, a new positive image of Patricia emerged,

Because of an early marriage and children, Patricia had never worked outside the home. With a new image of herself she was able to find a job as an office receptionist in a creative communications firm. She continued to visualise and focus upon her positive abilities. These brought her recognition by others and self-acceptance.

She is now a executive, independent and happy, with a career in which she contributes her skills of communications and creativity to a new self-awareness given to her by the SICA. This metamorphosis from an insecure, motherly, yet childlike, unhappy female, to a secure positive woman, occurred in a few short months. The SICA helped Patricia to find a purpose for living.

A BROKER TURNED MANAGER

At the time that John came to my office for an image consultation, he was a sales representative for a large financial brokerage house. The market was depressed and so was he. The SICA confirmed his feelings about himself. It also projected that his strengths to focus upon were his 'executive' (dark blue), circle 2, abilities, and his circle 1, honesty and 'lean upon me' qualities (brown). Others recognised his strengths, and he needed to image these daily to change his lacklustre outlook on life. John enjoyed his SICA and felt motivated by it.

Being in a large boardroom of forty or more brokers, some with spirits low, had been a difficult environment for positive imaging. With renewed zeal he planned to move ahead. He imaged himself in new colours, wearing mainly dark blues and browns. He changed his environment to earth tones, even placing a large piece of petrified wood on his desk. He worked with his new insights concerning his strengths. Fame, recognition, and monetary stability were his results, circle B (orange), a satisfied desire.

Today he is the manager of the same brokerage house and a motivated executive to hundreds of salespersons. John is up, the market is stabilising, and our manager includes gold in his rainbow spectrum.

AN UNDECIDED TURNED FOCUSED

A man named Richard was referred to me by a politician for whose campaign I had designed colours. He was seeking insight into himself simply because he did not know which direction to take. He was making various career choices in business and politics. His 'yuk' colour, circle 6, was black, yet he was wearing a favourite black suit to image himself. His SICA portrayed strong organisational qualities, circle 1 (orange), and balance with independent executive abilities, circle 3 (dark blue). He wanted a communicative challenge, circle 7 (yellow), and was desirous of change, circle B (apple green). His secret desire was to build and organise a new project, circle G (orange).

Richard found his new adventure, his new challenge, and a new freedom. He became leader, circle 1 (red), and communicator, circle 2 (yellow), of a political group where he could use his executive and organisational talents (dark blue and orange). This career change brought many rewards into his life restoring his sense of purpose and self-satisfaction. SICA not only aided Richard with his own image (not wearing the black suit), circle 6 (black), but gave additional insight that helped him find a self-rewarding career.

A TEACHER TURNED BUSINESSWOMAN

Burnout – a result of giving too much time and energy without financial or emotional reward – is one of the main stresses of the educator. Jane had such a problem. She was ready to leave her teaching job. Her SICA showed too much giving, circle 6 (pink), and not enough recognition, circle B (orange), as well as strong aspects of creativity, circle 2 (light blue). What Jane needed was to wear less pink in her wardrobe, and to introduce more greens and peaches to balance her stress, circle 6 (pink). She was yearning for a creative hobby to stimulate herself.

After SICA, Jane signed up for an evening real estate course in the area. Although she could only sell part-time, she became so motivated with her new profession that she started her own real estate business.

Successful today, she not only instructs her clients on home and property buying, but she designs courses for inexperienced realtors on how to listen to the needs of their clients. Financially rewarded, her income matches that of highly paid executives. But her greatest reward is her knowledge that she is creative (light blue).

A SALESPERSON TURNED SUCCESSFUL

Carol had spent a great deal of time and money on books, courses, and tapes on positivity to enhance her sales career. After a job change from secretary to salesperson, she was seeking a new image. Other females in similar professions were wearing dark, sombre outfits. Her SICA portrayed her in warm sunshine colours, circle 1 (yellow), circle 2 (orange), and circle 3 (gold). Unsure of how these new colour selections would help create sales, she hesitantly purchased a new outfit in shades of gold. Her colours imaged communication (yellow), organisation (orange), and successful accomplishments or high attainments (gold) for her balance. She liked her new image of herself.

In her first six months she doubled her production levels, and by the end of the same year she was chosen as the most productive sales executive for a large insurance company. Several articles have been written on her sales ability, her attitude, and her unique image. Carol credits the SICA with paving her road to success.

A STUDENT TURNED DIRECTED

SICA reinforces what we already know about ourselves. For a twenty-year-old college student, confused about his professional direction, SICA provided insight. Insecure, circle A (brown), and frustrated, circle F (orange), this student, Bill, came to my office for help. His profile showed positive strengths of creativity, circle 1 (light blue), and love of the earth and environments, circle 3 (brown). He was rebelling at the system, his 'yuk' colour, circle 6 (purple). He liked engineering, circle 4 (orange), but his major in college was English.

Recognising himself through his colour self-portrait, he decided to change his study curriculum. Now, with a degree in mining engineering and happily married, he has a career that he loves. His creativity (light blue) is expressed in development of practical uses for by-products of mines. His wife, a professional craftswoman in pottery, specialises in rainbow glazes.

From a confused, misdirected student to a satisfied mining engineer (orange and brown) who has found his inventiveness (light blue), this young man has followed his rainbow SICA.

A NURSE TURNED EXECUTIVE

Cindy, a nurse, completed her first SICA after an eight-hour shift on a hospital medical ward. Emotionally unrewarded, she was seeking change. In her frustration she thought that she was totally unskilled and unequipped to follow any other career except nursing. What to do was her question. SICA identified her as: a humanitarian, circle 1 (green), seeking change and challenge, circle B (apple green), and frustrated, her 'yuk' colour, circle 6 (orange). Her strengths showed the executive, circle 2 (dark blue), and the communicator, circle 3 (yellow).

She accepted her self-profile and changed her colours from whites, greens, and light blues to golds, yellows, dark blues, and peaches. Since her father had had a successful sales career, she began seeking a similar position.

A major corporation hired her as a counsellor and a sales representative in their tax division. Her image changed from a 'scrubbed too clean' female to a gracious, attractive person. Her executive peers were unconvinced that this beautiful woman was ever a plain Jane. Happy and successful, she found her humanitarian purpose and pursuit. Self-respect and a positive image were hers! She counsels others on how their image can aid them in solving their problems. Her SICA remains as the change agent that opened the door for a new beginning.

4

Colours for You

NOW that you have interpreted your SICA, you can make use of your colour selections for your wardrobe planning. Fashion designers and colour consultants usually classify colours by warms and cools, by contrasts, by intensities, and by design and style. In this chapter your clothing colours will be given as 'energy colours' to support you, who you are, and most important, to make you feel good.

Personal image counsellors claim that a person's social/ economic status can be determined by his or her clothing. So much emphasis has been placed on this initial impression created by one's appearance that a flood of information on how to 'dress for success' is now available in books, magazines, and even videos. Empirical studies have documented that both attire and colour make a personal statement, often adding to a credible professional image. Many researchers agree that a person's style of dress expresses the individual personality and gives clues to their probable social and behavioural interaction. Imagine how much more 'successful' you can be if your wardrobe is expressing the real you, and not what someone *else* thinks you should be!

You have expressed yourself through the language of

YOUR SELF-PORTRAIT

Chart I	Chart II

Colour ( ) 1   Colour ( ) A

Colour ( ) 2   Colour ( ) B

Colour ( ) 3   Colour ( ) C

Colour ( ) 4   Colour ( ) D

Colour ( ) 5   Colour ( ) E

Colour ( ) 6   Colour ( ) F

Colour ( ) 7   Colour ( ) G

colour, SICA! Now, whatever you want to declare about yourself, your strengths, your feelings, or your creative talents, your chosen colours from your SICA can make that statement. They'll extend a positive image of yourself, give you additional vitality, and act as your personal resource. As an aid to work, they'll support your energy and stamina to get you happily through the day.

Always match your colours to your feelings. When you prepare to dress, touch the outfit that you plan to wear with your left hand. For a moment permit yourself to feel the energy sensation of the colour. You can experiment each morning with this 'energy feeling' and with practice become very sensitive to the different vibrations of colour. If you have difficulty feeling the colour sensation, try direct eye contact with each colour outfit to receive the same sensation. By following these methods you will 'dress for (your own) success'. All colours that you wear will be positive energy, like sunshine to resource you.

Consider how colours react with you, day versus night. You feel different at your job than you do at home. Not only is it always smart to change your clothing and colours after a day at work, but it's also beneficial to your health and peace of mind. Colour is like a stimulant, and you can overdose with it, similar to overeating. That's why it's unwise to dress anytime in just one solid colour or to wear one colour all day long. Better for you to coordinate your outfits mixing and matching two or three colours together, and if you do happen to wear one colour all day, quickly get out of it as soon as you get home. Many people enjoy wearing solid black, yet without a helper colour, their image is so strong and severe that there's little flow of energy and interaction with others. They can feel depressed or 'down' by the end of the day. But wearing a little white, red, pink, or grey with their 'basic black' will change their feelings surprisingly. Another common mistake is the wearing of total white, with loneliness as the by-product. A red belt, scarf, shoes, jewellery, or purse will solve the 'alone' image problem, and the wearer will not only be individualistic but sexy too!

Learning to use SICA for wardrobe planning is very simple. All you have to do is to select personal colours from your intuitive self-portrait and incorporate them into your outfits. To devise an easy plan for recognising what your 'energy communication' colours are, jot down a Colour Clothing Plan according to your lifestyle requirements. This plan maps personal Colours for Work, Colours for Play, Colours to Present Oneself Positively, and Colours for greater Protection and Endurance against stresses.

COLOUR CLOTHING PLAN

COLOURS FOR WORK

According to your job, whatever it is – home, office, sales, or factory – you'll require colours that aid you to have a good day and be productive. You'll want to use your personal SICA colours to help you feel the best while extending the most positive image of yourself.

Start with Chart I of your SICA and select:

Colour No. 1 . . . (your identity-image colour)
Colour No. 2 . . . (your inspiration colour)
Colour No. 3 . . . (your balance colour)
Colour No. 4 . . . (your extended-image colour)
Colour No. 7 . . . (your motivation colour)

In choosing colours for daily outfits, begin with your *inspiration* and *balance* colours. These two colours are vital in your wardrobe! There are many shades of these colours, whether muted or vivid, so choose from the varied tints out there the ones that are most pleasing to you.

Your *inspiration* choice, colour No. 2, will give you a pick-me-up, aiding you to feel good during the day.

COLOURS FOR WORK

Chart I

Colour   1   ◯

Colour   2   ◯

Colour   3   ◯

Colour   4   ◯

Colour   5   ◯

Chart II

Colour   B   ◯

Colour   E   ◯

Your *balance* choice, colour No. 3, is a support colour, as it helps you feel secure and safe for the day.

Since you have imaged yourself as your *identity* colour, colour No. 1, there's no need to wear this colour as your dominant outfit colour, or to wear it all the time. You might use it more as an accent or secondary colour to the major colour of your outfit, such as in a blouse or tie.

The other colours of your SICA, colour No. 4, your *extended-image* colour, and colour No. 7, your *motivation* colour, can be worn to boost and support your image identity. So you may wear them as often as you please.

Once you have jotted down your five basic SICA colours for *work*, ask yourself a few more questions to help in designing your perfect-image wardrobe. 'What colours do I usually like to wear? Are my favourite colours the same as my SICA colours?' If you know what 'seasonal colour' type you are, are the colours of SICA similar?

Take some time to look in your closet to discover what colours you have already. Or decide what colours can be used to mix and match with your *inspiration*, your *balance*, your *extended-image* and *identity*, and your *motivation* colours.

From Chart II you'll find that two of your sensing and feeling colour choices can also contribute to your Colours for Work plan.

Colour B . . . (your intuitive-need colour)
Colour E . . . (your intuitive inner-strength colour)

Your sensing colour, colour B, may also act as a strong benefit, not only to give you more energy for the day and uplift your attitude, but also to help you to feel better about yourself. Colour B, your *need* colour is such a colour. Need colours are lucky colours; sometimes lucky for love, lucky for success, and lucky for new opportunities. You can use them to increase your positive outlook and your personal productivity. And of course, this colour adds to your personal satisfaction.

A good soothing colour for those hectic days at work is

COLOURS FOR PLAY

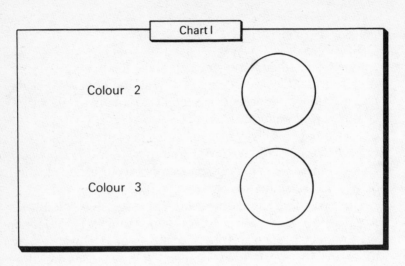

Chart I

Colour 2

Colour 3

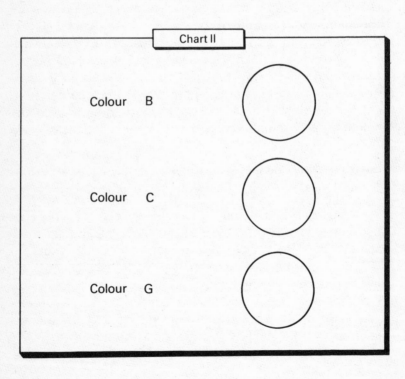

Chart II

Colour B

Colour C

Colour G

COLOURS TO PRESENT YOURSELF POSITIVELY

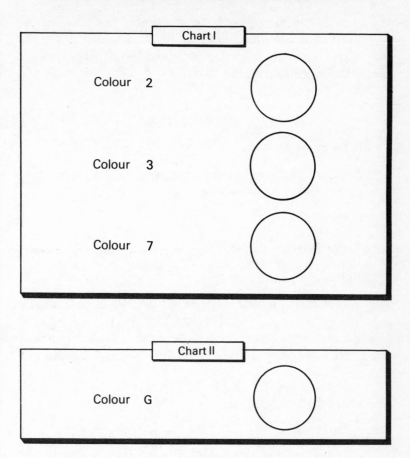

Chart I

Colour 2

Colour 3

Colour 7

Chart II

Colour G

COLOURS FOR PROTECTION & ENDURANCE

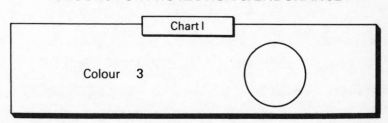

Chart I

Colour 3

colour E, your *inner-strength* colour choice. Wear it, keeping in mind that it communicates the 'together you' at work or play. This colour can help you use your energy properly as it keeps you peaceful and calm all day.

COLOURS FOR PLAY

From Chart I select:

Colour No. 2 . . . (your inspiration colour)
Colour No. 3 . . . (your balance colour)

From Chart II select:

Colour B . . . (your need colour)
Colour C . . . (your sweet colour)
Colour G . . . (your happy colour)

The colours that you have chosen for No. 2, No. 3, B, C, and G are all wonderful colours to play in and have a good time. You might find that you have chosen the same colour more than once, and if so, this colour is a 'must' for your playful outfits.

COLOURS TO PRESENT YOURSELF POSITIVELY

From Chart I select:

Colour No. 2 . . . for outfit, or accent such as blouse or tie
   or
Colour No. 3 . . . for outfit, or accent such as blouse or tie
Colour No. 7 . . . for accent
Colour G . . . for accent

COLOURS FOR PROTECTION AND ENDURANCE

From Chart I select:

Colour No. 3 . . . any dark or bright shade of this colour

As mentioned previously, your choice for colour No. 3 helps you to feel strong, safe, and secure. If for any reason you tire of wearing this colour a lot, you might want to choose another securing colour to add to your wardrobe. Following will be a chart of protection colours to help you make an alternative choice to your colour No. 3. You might even want to select more than one. The choice is yours.

PROTECTION COLOURS

Your protection colours may be used as your SICA colour No. 3, your *balance* colour, for they give added security when you place yourself in stressful situations, or ones that overtax your endurance levels. For example, when travelling short or long distances, your colours can aid as a source of protection from outside stresses and intrusion from large crowds. Many people become fatigued and stressed commuting on the motorways between home and office, when travelling by airplane, and on long vacation trips. Particularly for you salespersons who travel every week, your protection clolours are the right ones to be used on these occasions. At other times you can use these colours for added support and reinforcement on the job. When wearing a dark or bright colour, you will discover that you will feel stronger from the intensity of your clothing colour. Instead of saying 'I've had it', your protection colour becomes your 'I feel strong, safe, and secure' message.

RED   Counteracts physical fatigue
(Scarlet, cherry, or
Chinese red)

PINK   Relaxes mental tension
(Hot pinks,
magentas, or
plums)

MAROON (Wines, burgundies, or cranberry reds)	Protects from outside intrusions
ORANGE (Burnt orange, rust, or gingers)	Balances confusion
PEACH (Apricot, coral, or salmons)	Protects from energy loss
YELLOW (Honey yellows, lemon, or sunshine yellows)	Balances depression
MINT GREEN (Aqua, light turquoise, or sea greens)	Calms down emotional stress
APPLE GREEN (Celery, earth- or olive green)	Counteracts nervousness
GREEN (Kelly, leaf, or spring-grass greens)	Counteracts emotional stress
BLUE-GREEN (Teal, emerald, or evergreen)	Protects from outside interferences
LIGHT BLUE (Bright blue, turquoise, or peacock blue)	Prevents emotional draining

DARK BLUE (Royal blue, navy, or midnight blue)	Protects against failures
MAUVE (Orchids, rose plum, or rose beige)	Reduces stressful worrying
PURPLE (Grape, blue-violet, or plum purples)	Reduces outside pressures
BROWN (Dark brown, sienna, or earth browns)	Protects against insecurities
BLACK (Warm or cool blacks)	Protects against emotional over-sensitivity
WHITE (Antique or cream whites)	Releases over-burdening
GREY (Charcoal, stone, or silver greys)	Counteracts over-involvement
SILVER (Metal or pewter)	Protects against loss of self-worth
GOLD (Metallic or gold colours)	Counteracts loss

Whatever the shade of colour, light or dark, the vibrations of colour in your clothing help you. If you are concerned about how to wear certain colours because of how you look in them, don't be. For example, a pale yellow releases the same yellow sensation as a muted or golden yellow. If you're a person who has chosen yellow as one of your choices in your SICA, and you feel you simply can't wear most shades of yellow for they don't go with your skin, you might try an ivory yellow. You'll find a yellow to choose from, so don't omit yellow from your wardrobe palette.

Don't forget that your *motivation* and *inspiration* colours can be worn anytime as accent colours. They may be worn on the top or on the bottom in externally worn apparel, or even as undergarments. There are so many colours in undergarments out there to select from, so you can even wear your inspiration or motivation colours without others viewing them, which can help particularly if you have to wear a uniform or have a dress code at work. You might enjoy adding other motivational or inspirational colours to your wardrobe to give you an added boost when needed. The following charts will give you more insights into their energy messages.

MOTIVATION COLOURS

A motivation colour inspires goals, enhances relationships, and stimulates greater productivity. This colour may be worn as a gem or jewel, a scarf, a tie, or as an accent colour to any outfit. Your motivation colour will inspire you to direct a new flow of energy that expands both your image and personal goals. Motivating colours are ideal for pick-me-up days as they stimulate attitudes and feelings of self-worth. When you have those feelings of the 'blahs', when nothing feels quite right, call upon a motivating colour to change your mood.

Colour	Motivates:
RED	A strong image
PINK	Responsibility
MAROON	Self-love

ORANGE	Action and results
PEACH	Charity to others
YELLOW	Better communication
MINT GREEN	Self-awareness
APPLE GREEN	Change
GREEN	Clearer insight
BLUE-GREEN (teal)	Independence
LIGHT BLUE	Creativity
DARK BLUE	Wisdom and discernment
MAUVE	Personal intuition
PURPLE	Regal assuredness
BROWN	Stability
BLACK	Strength of convictions
WHITE	An individualistic image
GREY	A self-protective image
SILVER	Self-worth
GOLD	Material security

INSPIRATION COLOURS

Your *inspiration* colours are those colour choices from your SICA colour No. 2 that make you feel 'up'. Creativity is the key for using these colours, as they are wonderful aids for fun, for romantic interactions, and for helping you enjoy yourself. Wear your inspiration colour as a scarf, informal or play clothes, as an evening dressy blouse or shirt, or just anytime when you feel like letting your controls go. Enjoy and feel free, knowing that your 'uplifting colour' will do the rest.

Colour	Wear it for:
RED	Physical restoration Emotional stimulation
PINK	Nurturing self Increasing friendships
MAROON	Rewarding self Being carefree
ORANGE	Self-organisation Motivation
PEACH	Expressing yourself Feeling energetic
YELLOW	Better communication Halting depression
MINT GREEN	Feeling calm Feeling carefree
APPLE GREEN	Stimulating new opportunities Feeling challenged
GREEN	Stimulating practicality Maintaining balance
BLUE-GREEN (teal)	Promoting independence Feeling optimistic
LIGHT BLUE	Stimulating creativity Increasing perception
DARK BLUE	Protecting the emotions Preventing fatigue
MAUVE	Stimulating intuitive awareness Calming inner confusion
PURPLE	Feeling regal Protecting from over-indulgence

BROWN	Ensuring feelings of security
	Stabilising inconsistent actions
BLACK	Encouraging self-control
	Promoting strength of
	convictions
WHITE	Relaxing tensions
	Increasing individuality
GREY	Alleviating stress
	Relaxation and rest
SILVER	Stimulating self-respect
	Alleviating self-pity
GOLD	Self-reward
	Motivating high ideals

YOUR 'YUK' COLOUR

Your 'yuk' colour, colour No. 6, is not a colour to wear. You have rejected this colour for it turns you off. Do you know that this colour actually causes you to feel physically weaker and less productive? When you hold your 'yuk' colour in your hand, it might feel cold to your touch. This is because your energy is resisting the sensation from the colour. Don't wear it, and don't use it in your environment. Even when you've found a good bargain on a magnificent outfit, don't buy it if the sale item is close to your 'yuk' colour. You'll never feel right in it!

During one of my workshops, an interested participant questioned how to handle a situation when one's 'yuk' colour is imposed by a dress code, or a rented apartment is furnished with their 'yuk' colour. You might be concerned about the same thing, now that you know that you reject the sensation from your 'yuk' colour. It is important to find a creative solution. In apparel, by wearing the opposite colour of your 'yuk' colour, you can cancel any disturbing effect. A neutralis-

COLOUR WHEEL

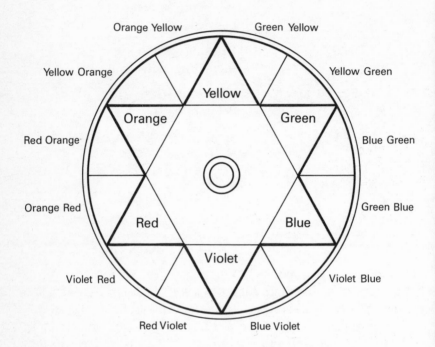

ing effect occurs when two opposite colours are put together. For example, shades of yellow cancel purple, blues cancel shades of orange, and any white, including ivory and bone, will erase the sensation of overall black.

As for a rented apartment that contains your 'yuk' colour, try the same creative technique that you might use in your wardrobe. Opposite colours when placed together give a neautralising or balancing effect. You can place a throw rug of maroon or burgundy on yellow-green carpet, or you might use throw pillows of a blue-red colour on your chartreuse lounge. Then add an accent of yellow to pull your whole colour scheme together. Instead of 'yuk,' your friends will say, how lovely!

Below is a chart showing you the opposite colours of the twenty SICA colours. Look for your 'yuk' colour choice, colour No. 6, then move across to find what opposite colour balances or neutralises it. Or you can look on the colour wheel on the inside back cover.

Colour	Opposite colour
RED	GREEN
PINK	DARK GREEN
MAROON	APPLE GREEN
ORANGE	BLUE
PEACH	DARK BLUE
YELLOW	PURPLE
MINT GREEN	CORAL
APPLE GREEN	MAROON
GREEN	RED
BLUE-GREEN (teal)	ROSE
LIGHT BLUE	RUST
DARK BLUE	PEACH
MAUVE	GOLD
PURPLE	YELLOW
BROWN	MINT GREEN
BLACK	WHITE
WHITE	BLACK

GREY ....NONE

SILVER ....GOLD

GOLD..SILVER

Because many of you look so good in your 'season hues' of colours, it's important to know how to blend your 'skin tone' colours with your SICA colours. In Carole Jackson's book, *Colour Me Beautiful*, she emphasises learning to select a personal wardrobe that contains shades of every colour to enhance your own natural colouring – skin, hair, and eyes. Her concept of 'seasonal colour' offers an easy guideline for dress. A Spring shines with clear, bright, or delicate colours having yellow undertones; a Summer flows with soft blues and pinks; an Autumn looks best in stronger hues or oranges, browns, and golds; and a Winter sparkles in bright, vivid, or icy colours with blue undertones.

If you know your season, take your colour palette and compare your seasonal colours to your SICA colours. They should not be contradictory. The SICA is your 'intuitive palette' and comes from within. Your SICA colours can easily be matched with personal shades of your 'season palette'. Your individuality and intuitive colour preferences not only strengthen your energy levels, but they add to your fashion-palette colours as well. Be not only well-dressed, but learn to wear colours that make you feel strong, balanced, and secure.

Many of my clients have asked for colour guidance on how to create a desired image. Fashion consultants, like most other professional authorities, often disagree on the exact methods of creating an image. Not disputing the theories of others, there is a simplistic method using only colours, not style or fashion of the day, as the principal designing rule. Below you will find these guidelines. You might even want to create some of your own, but remember, use only colour as your tool.

COLOURS FOR A DESIRED IMAGE

Here is the chart for coordinating two or more colours for contrast to project the image you want for the day, or for that special night.

Desired image:	Colours:
DRAMATIC	Bold, vivid, primary colours, strong contrasts. (Combine bold and strong colours)
ROMANTIC	Pinks, rose reds, and pastels of all red and violet shades. (Combine soft pastels, especially rose and pink colours. No sharp contrasts)
EXECUTIVE	Dark shades of blue, grey, brown, wine, and purple. All blacks with light pastel blouses or shirts. Bright colour accents only with scarves or ties. (Mix and match dark outfits with the lightest of coordinates with just a dash of colour)
SECURED	Earth tones and dark shades of all colours. (Combine earth tones or deep shades of colours with bright accents of gold, ivory, or white)
INTELLECTUAL	Blues, blue-greys, and muted blues or blue-greens. (Combine any shade of blue or blue-grey, with the basic neutrals, such as light grey, beige, or off-whites. Use stripes or linear designs in scarves or ties)
SENSUAL	All warm colours (except yellow); light, bright, and dark shades, especially reds.

(Combine colours using a dominant red or rose red with flashy contrasting jewellery)

PASSIVE   Greys and neutral shades of grey-browns and blue-greys.
                 (Combine the basic neutrals, such as grey or beige, with other muted greyed colours. Avoid sharp contrasts)

PROTECTIVE   Navy blues, dark browns, and blacks only.
                 (Combine these colours with small amounts of primary colours for accents)

HOLISTIC   Greens, violets, yellows, and earth tones with rainbow colours.
                 (Combine any greens with earth tones or any violets with golds or yellows or any basic colours with rainbow accents)

SUCCESS   All you SICA colour choices.
                 (Combine your skin-tone hues with your SICA colours of *inspiration, balance, identity*, and *inner strength*. Even try your *need* colour) Be yourself!

Last, but not least, in addition to SICA's help for wardrobe planning, I would like to mention a colour 'support method' for stress management. The book, *Creative Wellness, A Holistic Guide to Total Health*, by Michelle Lusson, deals both with the physical and psychological levels of health. Colour avoidance is one of the emphasised aids to this wellness support plan. The theory is that certain colours weaken one's resistance to stress according to individual glandular imbalances. If you're a person with physical problems such as a thyroid imbalance, allergies, or blood sugar irregularities, there are certain colours that should be avoided in your wardrobe. These colours further aggravate your glandular vulnerabilities, as they stimulate various personality traits, thereby overburdening your body's natural balance. For example, if you have problems with your thyroid, you might avoid red or blue-reds in outfit tops, as they stimulate a false sense of energy satisfaction, and less sensitivity to your own needs. I highly recommend this book for any of you who are experiencing a body weakness or physical irregularity. It should help you not only to know yourself better, but to stay healthy.

Experience now for yourself how your SICA colours and their energy qualities can be supportive to your wardrobe and you. If you've chosen a colour that isn't present yet in your closet, give yourself a treat and see what your intuitive colour can do for you.

5

Colours for Better Communication

DEFINING communication isn't easy; the scope is so great, the form and energy almost too irregular to lay down neat borders. My Merriam-Webster dictionary defines 'communication' as 'an act of transmitting; an exchange of information, a message.' This meaning is true, yet there's no mention of the human-energy factor of exchange. The usual person-in-the-street defines 'communication' as 'Let's talk' or 'Let me tell you what is happening with me' or 'Tell me, what's going on with you?'. This interaction is real, a true exchange of energy. Such is the interaction that takes place in colour communication. You don't need perfect English, the proper words, or even the right thing to say, but you do require the best colour for clear interaction. Colours communicate, they signal and send messages.

To accept the idea of colour as a message transmitter, take a look at some of the more common, accepted knowns. Red says 'Let's be physical', 'I'm strong', or 'Let's put our hearts together'. Rarely do we receive a 'mental' impression to red. Red often sends another signal: 'compete to the end'.

Imagine a boardroom meeting of executives where an important decision concerning company growth is about to take place. The attire emphasises the individuals' unspoken attitudes. Around the conference table sit four men and two women. The scene opens. Two of the board members are dressed in navy blue, two in grey, one in earth tones, and the other in red. How would you write the outcome of the meeting? An objective decision must be agreed upon by all. Five of the colours communicate support, while red signals an emotional response. The wearing of this colour may distract the other decision-makers. In an important meeting, colours worn by attending members are of the utmost significance. They may determine the outcome, and in this case, the future of the company.

Yellow expands and, when worn, opens better communications. Many of us empathise with the predicament of having children who resist attending new schools, beginning new projects, participating in instructions for art, music, or sports activities. I often wish that when I had young children I had known about the power of colour as a communicator. Yellow could have helped me, because I had a shy child who had difficulty returning to school after summer holidays. He just hated to make new friends. A yellow shirt might have reduced his feelings of shyness. Since he liked yellow and had some favourite tops in this colour, wearing them might have helped him overcome his shyness.

For expanding your ability to communicate, try yellow; a yellow scarf, belt, blouse, or tie will do the trick. Yellow is the non-verbal mouth!

The favourite of all colours is the popular blue. In fact, in the history of colour, the more technologically oriented a culture, the more people preferred blue. In these societies you'll see it as the number one car, the number one suit, and always, the colour most preferred by men. Why? Blue, in all shades, communicates 'I love my mind, and I like to be logical and practical'. I theorise that blue is the colour of the left brain, as it indicates intellect, not feeling. Messages signalled by the colour blue always pertain to the mind, for it calms our emotions, which then sets our minds free. The language of blue, then, echos the tone of modern society. In business situations, blue always gives strong support; however, too much blue on the body can have a negative side effect, as it reduces libido, our physical energy. Those of you who work in exacting professions, such as accounting, computers, or secretarial work, require extra energy support for your bodies, not minds. Blue is not the best for you, except in shades of navy, as navy is a high-energy supportive colour. Bright red won't help either, since it will focus all your energy on the needs of your body. You might settle for an in-between colour to help you with better communications. Try a basic neutral with a bright primary colour accent or one of your favourite earth tones with a blue accent. Remember, blue supports the mind for it images the intellect. But don't forget your body; you need it also.

On the following pages are two charts; the first will translate the *communicative message* of each colour; the second will identify situations where colours present the clearest non-verbal signals. Look up your favourite colours and see which message they are sending. Learn how your wardrobe colours become better than a dicitionary definition for 'communication.' And it's important; your colours are not separate from you; together you are one communicative message.

CHART I

Colour Communicative Messages

Colour	Message
RED	'Look at me, I'm physical and emotional.'
PINK	'I like to love, be loved, and care for others.'
MAROON	'I want to play and have a little fun.'

ORANGE	'I'm organised and like to accomplish my goals.'
PEACH	'I'm charitable, kind, and like to be involved.'
YELLOW	'Let's communicate, I like to share.'
MINT GREEN	'I'm practical, calm, and like harmony in my life.'
APPLE GREEN	'I like challenges and I want to be different.'
GREEN	'Give me your sick and needy, for I like to help them.'
BLUE-GREEN (teal)	'I'm always the optimist, and I have faith in others.'
LIGHT BLUE	'Let me show you how creative yet analytical I am.'
DARK BLUE	'I love to be the boss and the decision-maker.'
MAUVE	'I'm very intuitive, yet I need encouragement always.'
PURPLE	'I like to express my feelings and have others recognise how great I am.'
BROWN	'Let me show you with my hands, for I am industrious and love my work.'
BLACK	'Don't tell me what to do, for I know best.'
WHITE	'I like to be by myself, even in a crowd, for I need my own space.'
GREY	'I hear what you say, but I don't want to be involved.'
SILVER	'I'm a romantic who likes to feel good about myself.'

GOLD   'I want everything, money, power, and to sit
                on top of the world.'

Colour communication sends non-verbal signals. We exhibit our needs by the colours we wear. For example, one who wears red a lot might be looking for a new love relationship, or attempting to restore their physical endurance. You might ask if it's necessary to know what you want before you wear the colour, as many of you have friends and associates who like to wear certain colours but have no idea of what they want or why they're wearing a particular hue a lot. To answer that question, you only have to compare non-verbal body language to the language of colour. If a person crosses their arms while listening to a speaker, although they are unaware that their body is sending signals, a message is sent, one of probable rejection of the speaker's words.

A craving or desire for a colour sends a clear non-verbal message too! It signals a want or need, one that wishes to be satisfied with the use of a certain colour. As an example, when you find yourself over-extended in time and energy, you might develop a craving for or find yourself wearing grey all the time. Or you may see your friend who wants to be more independent buying a new teal sweater. Both situations send colour non-verbal messages. Colour, come to my aid!

Below, you will find listed situations where colour presents the clearest non-verbal messages. To use, look up the colour that is being desired and read its communicative meaning.

CHART II

Communicate More Effectively

Colour	Wear When You Want To:
RED	Bring in a romantic relationship Restore your physical endurance Express greater power Stand out in a crowd
PINK	Rescue yourself from stress Energise your femininity Stimulate responsibility for others Relax your mind and listen to your heart
MAROON	Reward yourself with some fun Stimulate a sensual relationship Ward off outside stresses Protect yourself from draining persons
ORANGE	Organise your time and energy Motivate yourself Bring in a desired result Protect your physical stamina
PEACH	Enhance your charitable action Support your energy levels Show love in action Stimulate the good opportunities
YELLOW	Enhance your communicative abilities Halt or prevent depression Stimulate your desires Sell yourself and your skills
MINT GREEN	Calm your emotions Heal your body Reduce outside drains Stimulate your romantic dreams

APPLE GREEN	Renew your desires
	Motivate new interests
	Stimulate a challenge
	Bring a new opportunity

GREEN	Motivate your objectivity
	Promote health consciousness
	Stimulate an independent goal
	Calm your emotional response to discord

BLUE-GREEN (teal)	Promote your independence
	Stimulate your practicality
	Maintain spiritual practices
	Reduce emotional stresses

LIGHT BLUE	Stimulate your creativity
	Encourage your learning
	Calm down over-activity
	Increase your logic and analytical insight

DARK BLUE	Protect your emotions
	Prevent fatigue on the job
	Enhance your wisdom and discernment
	Stimulate your self-awareness

MAUVE	Stimulate your intuitive insights
	Trust your feelings
	Calm your inner confusion
	Reduce over-activity

PURPLE	Believe more in your faith
	Protect from over-involvements
	Stimulate your intuitive abilities
	Reduce outside pressures

BROWN	Ensure inner feelings of security
	Prevent weight loss
	Calm down excessive mental activity
	Stabilise inconsistent actions

BLACK   Protect from outside influences
             Release unknown fears
             Encourage self-control
             Promote your strength of convictions

WHITE   Counteract negative thinking
             Communicate an individualistic image
             Reduce your muscular tension
             Be open to new ideas

GREY   Alleviate outside stresses
             Prevent unnecessary involvements
             Encourage a self-protective image
             Promote a calm, passive countenance

SILVER   Inspire faith and hope
             Increase self-worth and self-esteem
             Stimulate self-respect
             Protect from inner fears

GOLD   Increase your material success
             Motivate high ideals
             Stimulate desire for self-reward
             Enhance feelings of security

The subject of colour communications offers one more very important transmitting and receiving avenue, one that gives us insight into our relationships with each other. But this method is the most difficult to grasp. You'll become your own analyst, so you are the one who sets the platform. Your *identity colour* will be your player.

Draw a circle in the middle of a clean white page. This becomes your sun, and the centre of your universe. Place your identity colour in your sun. Continue, with radiating lines to smaller circles surrounding your sun. Add the number of circles of persons in your family, or the number of circles representing peers and associates on the job. Now you have your personal or professional universe.

101

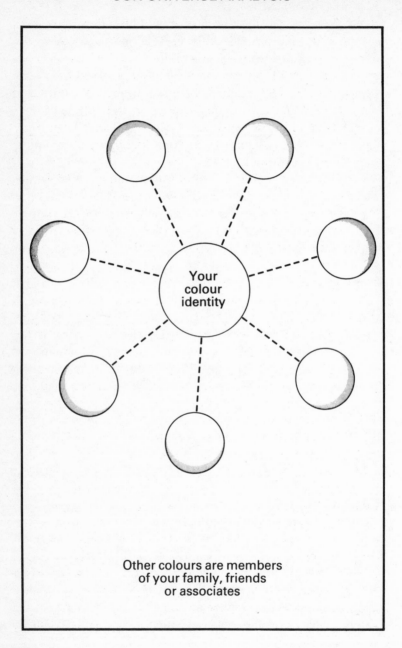

Other colours are members
of your family, friends
or associates

Ask someone what colour they would be if they could be a colour. This will help identify their relationship to you. It will be fun to ask your spouse, your children, your close friends, or even your boss or any person who has a personal or professional influence in your life. Target their individual circles, and place their name and identity colour in the centre of each circle. Your universe becomes a rainbow. Don't have more than ten circles radiating from your identity colour, unless your family is extremely large.

Colours foster better communication among our family, friends, and workmates. Identity similarities, like colours in a painting, can work together to create a harmonious design, or one that is lacking in harmony. Colours can show how to encourage a better relationship with another, or they can show a discord.

The radiating circles around your identity colour will give you insight into your interaction with others. For example, if your identity colour is red, and you have other warm colours, such as pink, maroon, orange, peach, yellow, or brown in the orbiting circles, you enjoy like qualities and strengths in the people around you. All warm colours are expressive, energetic, emotional, and extroverted. Your common denominator, the warm colour, represents a desire to express, and especially to communicate with mouth, hands, emotions, and body. You'll find that all colours that are similar to your identity colour express aspects of you.

Let's say, for example, that you identify as yellow, and you discover that among your family two have chosen the same colour, yellow, one has chosen dark blue, one light blue, one peach, and one mauve. Immediately you'll recognise that the yellows are communicative like you, always talking, and the peach is charitable, enjoys giving. The dark blue intellectualises, the light blue likes to create and image with the mind, and the mauve is gentle but intuitive. The yellows will have to be quiet to listen to the blues and the mauve. The peach will readily give time to the yellows. The blues will let the yellows express themselves, and the mauve will need some quiet time to be intuitive and listen to their feelings. Then the yellows can interpret the mauve to the blues and so on. See how easy colour identity for better communications can be, especially with a family.

Look up in the chart below the description for the colour identity of those you wish to communicate better with. If your identity colour is one of the blues, you can understand other cool colours such as green and purple. You'll see like qualities in these colour identities. Blues think and analyse with the mind, and they act out more subdued communications and interactions. Greens also like to use their minds before their emotions and mouths, while mauves and purples like to be quiet but use their minds too. What the cool colours have in common are like qualities of enjoying thinking faculties. But they usually need at least one red to keep the energy flowing.

If you discover that all of the surrounding circles are not akin to your identity colour, you'll need to find alternative avenues to communicate clearly. Each colour will provide a means for new insights into a better interaction. In colour dynamics, a red always balances a green or blue-green, yellow helps purple to work more expressively, and blue governs or is supported by orange and brown. As identity colours of others interact with your identity colour, they'll complement or stimulate you. If not, you'll just have to put greater effort into enhancing your relationships.

Below is the chart for you to analyse all of the identity colours in your 'sun universe' drawing. Read the one word meaning for each colour and you'll find a new insight into the relationship between you and she or he. Your 'non-verbal colour communications' diagram will give you greater understanding of how a part of you enjoys relating more positively with others.

RED	Energetic
PINK	Loving
MAROON	Emotional
ORANGE	Conscientious
PEACH	Charitable
YELLOW	Communicative
MINT GREEN	Idealistic
APPLE GREEN	Innovative
GREEN	Benevolent
BLUE-GREEN (teal)	Optimistic
LIGHT BLUE	Creative
DARK BLUE	Intellectual
MAUVE	Intuitive
PURPLE	Sensitive
BROWN	Supportive
BLACK	Protective
WHITE	Individualistic
GREY	Passive
SILVER	Honourable
GOLD	Materialistic

Part Two

*COLOUR,
A NATURAL SUPPORT*

6

Colours for Your Personal Environment

FOR those of you who feel hesitant about calling upon an interior decorator, or don't have the financial means to hire one, colour-designing your own home or office can be a rewarding hobby. What makes a room really great is your personality and feelings of comfort. When it comes to style of furniture – antique, traditional, oriental, contemporary, or a harmonious blending of styles – all options are open. Your decorating will develop easily as you begin to feel secure with your colour choices. In any bookstore you can find a variety of 'how-to' books that describe principles for good design. But the most important rule for easy decorating is an understanding of how colours work to represent *you*.

Disregarding the 'in thing' fashion colour trends, you might intuitively select only those colours that are pleasing to your senses. As to the right use of colour, *you* are the best decorator for your environment. And besides, the results of your creativity will be very satisfying.

Take a walk through your home, pretending you're a professional designer, and think about what style best describes the person who lives there. Bold, elegant, conservative, traditional, or warm – which expresses the mood and feeling you most enjoy? Does your home express that feeling? Look carefully at your favourite room. Perhaps you like spending time there because the colours make you feel so good? Have you ever wondered why your spouse loves his favourite easy chair, or why you sleep better on warm pastel sheets than on the cooler blues? Consider the answers to all of these questions – they will provide important guidance for your selection of colours. And remember, your feelings will be the most important factor in colour choosing.

It is important therefore to use SICA, the language of colour, to help you determine what your personal colours are for your decorating needs.

ENVIRONMENTAL SICA

There are only three questions to answer. As a guide to help you visualise the colours, return to the twenty-colour selection display on the inside front cover. Also remember that you can choose any shade or tint of these colours, but select only one colour for each answer. Again, be intuitive for the best results.

Colour No. 1   *What colour gives you the most pleasing feeling?*
(Close your eyes, feel wonderful, all your senses are satisfied. What colour comes to mind?)

Colour No. 2   *What colour strengthens you?*
(Feel strong, everything around you is supporting you. What colour gives you that feeling?)

Colour No. 3   *What colour makes you feel most secure?*
(See yourself as totally fulfilled; you want for nothing, you have it all. What colour comes to mind?)

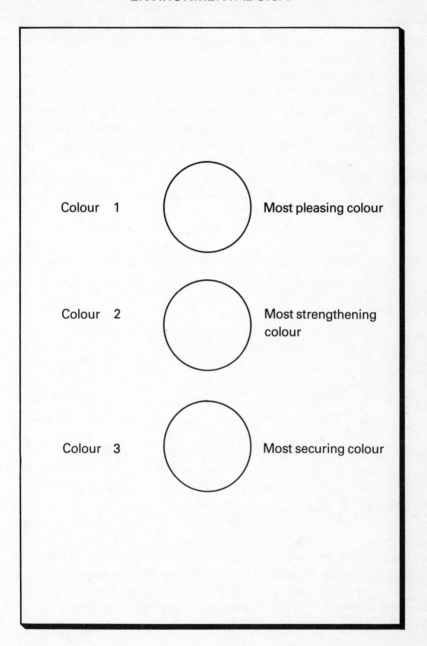

Once you have selected your colour choices, write them down, for they are your most comfortable and satisfying colours. They will guide you in determining what colours to use for your home!

Other members of your family play a vital role in home decorating. Ask each one what their favourite colour is, or give them the environmental SICA questionnaire. Surprisingly, you may find some members of your family enjoy the same colours that you feel good with. Be sure to include their colour preferences in various accents, such as a couch pillow, a drapery colour, or a creative ornament. Combine in your overall colour scheme hues that represent comfortable feelings of all members of your family.

Read now how to use your environmental SICA colours, and those of your family. It's not important to translate them into words or communicative messages, for their 'energy support' will be all that matters.

Colour simplicity means decorating for comfort! Combine your three colour choices into paint for your walls, any floor coverings or tiles, and colours of the patterns in your furnishings to set the stage for successful designing. For example, you might want to use a light shade of colour No.1 (your most pleasing colour) on your walls; try in a sofa or chair to use your colour No. 2 (your strengthening colour); and for a carpet, choose your colour No. 3 (your security colour). Tie them all together with interesting accent colours that complement your entire SICA colour scheme. You may even use for an accent colour your SICA identity colour No. 1 from your self-portrait.

Decide what you want your home to be – artistic, inviting, mellow, or dramatic. Then begin designing a room by using one colour as the dominant tone. You can find it in almost every shade from light to dark. Use another in furnishings, or in an accent wall covering or in your carpet colour tone. Your third colour choice will tie the colour design of colour No. 1 with colour No. 2 by adding additional harmony or contrast, or by simply introducing a secure feeling to the room.

If, for example, your environmental SICA colours are brown, light blue, and yellow, you might choose any shade of brown or tan for walls or carpeting. Then add complementary blue chairs or ones having blue and golden yellow designs. Finally, complete the colour design ingredients with yellow cushions or throw pillows. For added colour complement, look to find a painting with sun, sky, and earth. Your room will be perfect, pleasing, strengthening, and securing. Or maybe you'd like to select pale-ivory or yellow walls with blue and earth-tone furnishings and tie them together with a luxurious blue carpet. Make sure that your colours enhance your feelings, or you won't be happy later on. Your favourite rooms need to be welcoming, but most important, very livable for you. After all, aren't your colours a representation of you?

Top designers emphasise, 'Create your home as something very personal, the reflection of you.' Your living room, dining area, and kitchen represent your image. Like the image of your car or your favourite outfit, the colours in your home speak.

Once you've reflected on your personal colour choices, if you feel that there's still a colour problem in designing your home environment, or you're not quite satisfied with your 'feeling' colours, there are alternative ways to solve the problem using your personal self-portrait, SICA.

Return to your self-portrait and study the colours that you have chosen for Chart I. Ask yourself, 'Do I like the colours that I have chosen for Chart I?' Could you pick just three of them for decorating your home? After all, they are colours that extend your image. You may prefer them in your home as well. If you don't favour your 'feeling' colours, try your image colours, they'll work too. But don't use your 'yuk' colour in your home!

Another easy method for choosing colours for your home is to join with your spouse or friend, or whoever is your homemate, in selecting a painting or art design that has in its composition or subject matter colours that you both like and can live happily with. Ask yourselves if these colours please you and make you feel secure. Then choose three of the colours from the art piece for your personal colour scheme in designing your home. Build those 'pleasing feelings' around the colour of the art that you enjoy!

I have an interesting story to relate about a colour design problem involving a married couple, and how it was solved.

A few years ago a young lady telephoned the office, wanting to know if I could aid her in resolving a stressful situation. Apparently she and her husband had recently purchased a home, but they were unable to arrive at a mutual agreement concerning a basic colour scheme for decorating. The husband's favourite colour was blue, and he expressed a strong dislike for anything green. Her problem was that she loved greens and disliked blues. This problem typically occurs when people enter a new cycle of their lives, such as buying a new home. A seemingly small choice becomes a monumental obstacle.

The results of their joint participation in the SICA were revealing. The husband did indeed identify with shades of blue; his 'yuk' colour was green; while his wife, including her professional image, identified as green and suffered discomfort with too much blue. The key that opened the door for a happy decision was the colour gold. Both parties chose gold for security and feelings of comfort. The interior design colour scheme was then decided quite simply. A gold carpet throughout the home, antique off-white walls with golden highlights, furnishings coordinating golden yellows, muted green-blues, woods, straws, and green plants brought about the settlement of their differences. Indeed, their gratitude and pleasure remained in the aura of my office for many days.

Now you're ready to work with your colours to decorate. Read the helpful hints for colour decorating in the chart below, and become your own master designer. If you still feel unsure of yourself, ask for guidance from a professional, but don't forget your personal colours – they represent you!

SIMPLE WAYS TO COLOUR DECORATE

Here are a few ways to enjoy your favourite colours in individual rooms without struggling over design decisions. Start by creating a small room that you enjoy. Have your SICA colours offer their 'energy', while delighting your eyes at the same time.

1. Design 60 per cent of the room – walls and floor, whether it be carpet, tile, or wood – in various tints and shades of *one* favourite colour.

2. Make 30 per cent of the room – draperies and upholstered furniture – tints and shades of your *second* favourite colour.

3. Accent the final 10 per cent of the room – with pictures, vases, pillows – in colours to please and support all members of your household.

4. Repeat colours to unify a room or tie one room to another, for these colours if carried throughout the entire home later will build a coordinated image.

5. Remember, woods and other natural products are colours. Wood-tones, fibres, bricks, or stones are all part of your colour scheme, as they are part of the total picture of any room.

6. The lighting, both natural and artificial, in the room that you are designing affects your colours. Colours look different under daylight than they do under various kinds of artificial light or night lighting. Warm lights cause your warm colours to appear warmer, while cool lights will make your colours seem greyer; and the opposite will happen with your cool colours. If the rooms that you are decorating are very dark, do not choose your colours outside or in better-lit rooms. Rather, select the colours in the exact room to be designed.

7. Bright, bold primary colours, such as red, yellow, and bright blues, decrease the size of rooms. You might use these colours more for accents or in smaller pieces of furniture.

8. Light and pastel colours make a room look larger and lighter. You may want to use these colours for smaller rooms and areas. Pastel colours also help you relax.

9. White is a colour and should be considered as one of your three design colours. Remember, if you design with all white, your room can be lonely, so add two more colours to make it sparkle.

10. Use at least two different colours together in any room to create contrast. When you use a small amount of contrast with shades of the same hue or colour, your room will be more restful and calm, as well as airy.

11. Warm colours, such as reds, yellows, oranges, and browns, create warmer atmospheres in a room, conserving heat and electricity. Cool colours, such as blues, purples, and greys, chill down the temperature of the room and can be used as natural air conditioners. Warning: too much blue in any room might cause you to want to wear a sweater!

COLOURS FOR SPECIAL ENVIRONMENTS

You may want added knowledge on how to design nurseries, children's rooms, or rooms for the elderly. If you feel that a room requires particular attention in decorating, it is a special environment!

Let's address special environments one at a time, and if you find the information helpful to your personal requirements, try experimenting with it.

1) *From your child's birth until it is about age seven*, you, Mum, or you, Dad, are the designer. Your responsibility is not to over-activate your child's nursery or room with colour choice and bold contrasts. Bright, intense colours, such as bright reds, oranges, and strong yellows, can be over-stimulating, while light yellow, peach, or pink are more suitable, for they are soothing and comfortable. Greens are calming and cooling, yet are not always advisable for chilly rooms or for nurseries where baby is susceptible to colic or colds. It's true, blue has been identified as the colour for little boys, yet some blues are so cool that they can make a newborn feel the cold more. You can use blues positively to aid an over-active child, but don't count on it to offer much physical or emotional support. Try one of the other colours on the walls or your son's room with blue accents of furnishings and trims. In this way the room says 'boy child' but doesn't overdose with the cooling blues.

When you don't know your child's gender before birth, select a light yellow and, after the child is born, add a few bright accents for his/her identity. Your baby reacts favourably to soft light when born and grows in sensitivity to surrounding colours as he/she develops. Be communicative and warm with your young child, and later on in life, they will let you know how much they care.

2) *From age seven to age fourteen,* you, Mum and Dad, are the designers, with your child as your major consultant. Ask your child what his favourite colour is, and what colour makes him feel the best. Share his colour wants and encourage him to enjoy designing his room. If your son enjoys pink or purple, and your reaction is that it's not okay, don't feel that way, for your child is requesting a colour for a reason. Agree and acknowledge him. Shy, sensitive children of either sex love the gentle, intuitive colours. On the other hand, if your 'tomboy girl' is into bright reds and blues, recognise that she too wants her personal colours, and they're right for her. She may be

117

asking for more colour support to help her grow bright and strong.

3) *From age seventy to whatever*, you, as a respected senior, always require extra colour balancing and support. Especially when your feet are cold or you're having a depressing day, you can call upon colour to aid. Warm colours control cool environments, while soft yellow and salmons also prevent loneliness or depression. The myth that the elderly prefer violet is just that, a misbelief. In fact, violet or mauve is not the best choice for a senior citizen as it can cause an elderly person to become overly introspective and moody. For walls and accents in furnishings, the best colours are light pinks, salmons, yellows, blue-greens, and beiges. They can all work as helpers to promote comfort and security. So when one's hair turns to white, it's time to use more colour in the environment.

4) *The most influential room* to give special attention to is the bathroom. Romans and Greeks understood the attributes of the bath, that of rejuvenation and restoration. Think about it. Don't you enjoy spending time there, maybe even hours soaking and pampering? Your day begins in the bathroom. In order to get a good start there, make sure the colours are uplifting. Turn your bathroom into a magic spa for repairing that body of yours, and rejuvenating and putting on your face for the day. Your colours should inspire you as you get your first look at yourself. Instead of peering into your mirror with a long face, let your bathroom colours serve as your first 'pick-me-up'.

Naturally, when choosing the principal colour for your bathroom, start with an inspiring colour. Use any tint or shade of this colour. Design the accents of your bathroom with colours that represent other family members or associates, so that they will feel as good as you do. Listed below is a simple chart for inspiring colours.

COLOUR FOR BATHROOM DESIGNING

RED	Cherry, scarlet, or Chinese red – (PHYSICAL)
PINK	All pinks, hot pinks, and plums – (ROMANTIC)
MAROON	Wines, burgundies, or cranberry reds – (SENSUAL)
ORANGE	Tangerines, orange, or burnt orange – (STRUCTURED)
PEACH	Apricot, peach, or salmon – (EMOTIONALLY SUPPORTIVE)
YELLOW	Lemon or sunshine, and honey yellows – (CHEERY)
MINT GREEN	Sea green, mint, or aquas – (SOOTHING)
APPLE GREEN	Celery, grass, apple or nile greens – (EXCITING)
GREEN	Emerald, kelly or leaf greens – (HEALING)
BLUE-GREEN	Teal, ocean, or evergreens – (PEACEFUL)
LIGHT BLUE	Turquoise, baby or peacock blue – (SERENE)
DARK BLUE	Royal blue, navy or midnight blues – (EXECUTIVE)
MAUVE	Orchid, rose plum, or rose beiges – (FEELINGFUL)
PURPLE	Grape, blue-violet, or plum purples – (DIGNIFIED)

BROWN	Beige, tan, sienna, or earth browns – (SECURING)
BLACK	All shades of black – (MODERN, but SEVERE)
WHITE	All shades of white – (UNCLUTTERED, but STERILE)
GREY	Stone or silver and charcoal greys – (RESTFUL)
SILVER	Metallic or pewter silvers – (LUXURIOUS)
GOLD	Metallic or gold colours – (ELEGANT)

CHROMATIC PLANNING FOR JOB SUPPORT

Have you ever gone to work and wondered what you could do to have your job environment be more congenial and satisfying? Perhaps you've bought something new for your desk to liven it up a bit. Most of you who work for government or big business, or even services and sales organisations, have had little or no voice in designing your job environments. Fortunately there's growing interest among business to change the work environment, to include the needs of the employees and to make the surroundings more pleasing and efficient.

Home and office, like shelter and open space, often don't have the same focus of performance or purpose. When at home, we rest, relax, rejuvenate, and create, while on the job we work, produce, serve, and solve job-related problems, resting little if at all. Our 'energy' is consumed more at work than at home. This is not quite so true with many homemakers, since their role as mother and father requires the same endurance level as a full-time job. Wherever your energy is mostly spent, you could use a little extra help from the colours in your environment.

It's essential in order to receive the most benefit from your personal colours to place them somewhere within three feet of your working space. On a table, desk a chair, in a piece of art, or as an accent colour, anywhere in view – for your colours can act as strong energy to help you feel good and produce your best at work.

You might select your personal colours from your SICA self-portrait, colour No. 2, your inspiration colour, and colour No. 3, your balance or security colour. For example, if your balance colour is maroon, you can use it in your office as your desk chair, a wallpaper design, a small area rug, or even as a figurine on your desk. If it's not possible to have a say in the colours of your work environment, carry an object of maroon with you, like a pen that you can place on your desk while at work. Any object at all in a maroon colour can serve as your balance colour to help you feel better on the job. Try even a maroon scratch-pad holder, an ink blotter, or maroon vase. To gain the 'energy effect' from your personal colour, you don't have to have a lot of it, just a small amount to energise you through the day.

Your inspiration colour, No. 2 from your SICA, may be another colour you wish to include in your work environment. Let's suppose that you've chosen yellow. You can have it as a tablet, a book, a planter, a name tag, a favourite coffee mug, or any piece of office equipment around you. Like a friend, the colour yellow will support you to be more communicative and inspired while at work.

Some of my clients have asked what to do when their work environment is colour designed in their 'yuk' colour. Unfortunately this often happens and makes for a critical and immediate need for the resolution to the problem. The best way to handle your 'yuk' colour is to hastily add in your work space personal colours for additional support, and you should wear colours that neutralise the energy effect of your dislike colour. Refer back to the chapter Colours for You, to the section Your 'Yuk' Colour (page 87), and read how to cancel the effect of the colour with its opposite. Sadly, you may have to wear a lot of the same colour outfits, but at least you'll be feeling fine and producing at work.

Last but not least in this chapter, for all you business owners or entrepreneurs who might want to image your service or your products with communicative impressions from the meanings of colours, below is a list of colours for services and marketing. These, along with your personal SICA colours, may be used as accents, business cards, logos, signs, or creative designs for your company. Here are some definitions and examples of colour-imaging.

Colour	Service or Product Pertaining to:
RED	PHYSICAL IMAGING (Sports, exercise clubs, dining or dancing services, political clubs and organis- ations)
PINK	A FEMININE OR LOVING IMAGE (Fashions, cosmetics, rescuing services, church clubs, and infant services and products).
MAROON	GRATIFICATION OF THE SENSES (Entertainment, videos, cars furnishings, art services, gambling, and beverages)
ORANGE	HIGH-ENERGY IMAGES (Architecture, building tools and services, speedy services and efficiency products)
PEACH	CHARITABLE IMAGING (Services and products for children, schools products, welfare organisations or charities)

YOUR SELF-PORTRAIT

Chart I		Chart II	
Colour ◯ 1		Colour ◯ A	
Colour ◯ 2		Colour ◯ B	
Colour ◯ 3		Colour ◯ C	
Colour ◯ 4		Colour ◯ D	
Colour ◯ 5		Colour ◯ E	
Colour ◯ 6		Colour ◯ F	
Colour ◯ 7		Colour ◯ G	

YELLOW | COMMUNICATION
(Yellow Pages, all services and products of the communication and entertainment industries, especially sales)

BRIGHT GREENS | INNOVATIVE IMAGING
(Self-enhancement services and products, weight and diet centres, self-help services)

ALL GREENS | HEALTH, VEGETABLE, OR PLANT INDUSTRIES
(Health food stores, homey restaurants, floral products and services)

LIGHT BLUE | CREATIVE IMAGES
(Design or art industry, creative products or problem-solving services, computer products and servicing)

DARK BLUE | EXECUTIVE IMAGING
(Business, education, and executive products and servicing

MAUVE OR PURPLE | SPIRITUAL OR INTUITIVE IMAGING
(Training or services for emotional support. Sensitive imaging to the needs)

BROWN | SUPPORT PRODUCTS AND SERVICES
(Businesses offering security, basic-needs and survival products)

BLACK | AUTHORITY IMAGING
(Security or protection services. Sedate, severe, and aloof imaging)

WHITE | INDIVIDUALISTIC OR SANITARY IMAGING
(Better with products than services as it will give an image of 'aloneness')

GREY	PASSIVE OR EARTH-SUPPORT IMAGES (Home repair services and products, stone and earth products, but not to image any services relating to human resources)
SILVER	AN HONOURABLE AND WORTHY IMAGE (Legal services, money lending, and civil rights organisations)
GOLD	IMAGES OF SECURITY AND WEALTH (Brokers, bankers, merchants, and high-quality services)

7

Colour Energy, a Natural Support

(Colour guides for moods, attitudes, and feelings of well-being)

HAVE you ever begun the day feeling as if you've got up 'on the wrong side of the bed'? Nothing felt quite right. You needed a 'pick-me-up' colour to wear for the day. The vibrational energy of colour serves to change your mood as much as you will accept its service. Colours may even make you feel better about being alive, because they interact with you to perform whatever function is necessary. From depression, despair, or the 'blahs', colours can alter your attitude for the better. If colours are known to raise blood pressure (the reds), and calm over-active emotions (the greens), you can choose a colour that will answer your energy need for each day.

Wearing the right colours can aid, encourage, strengthen, and support you. As you've already discovered, some inspire, ensure, protect, and also can act efficiently as attitude-change tools. All serve you as good performance supports and ego boosters. Look at the following chart to find what colour can help you solve an attitude or mood problem for an extra boost each day.

In your wardrobe, use the colour as an accent, such as in a scarf, tie, or belt. If you want a larger amount of colour energy, try a mix-and-match coordinate such as a blouse or shirt, but don't wear it alone without a helper colour. All tints and shades of each hue work well as your attitude changer or 'pick-me-up' support.

Colour	Feeling or Attitude to Change:
RED	Lack of physical energy Lack of strength or courage Feeling of unwantedness or rejection Negative thinking
PINK	Lack of self-acceptance Inability to love or nurture others Insensitivity to your own needs Emotional traumas
MAROON	Not enough love of life Intolerance of others Fear of being ugly and unloved Emotional insecurities concerning involvements
ORANGE	Lack of vitality Lack of motivation Uncertainty as to personal direction Inability to achieve results
PEACH	Lack of energy Inability to stabilise your emotions Insensitivity to the needs of others Low blood sugar levels
YELLOW	Despair or depression Loneliness or feelings of being alone Lack of open communication Feelings of frustration or limitation

MINT GREEN	Uncontrolled anger Feelings of resentfulness Lack of emotional control Lack of patience
APPLE GREEN	Lack of new opportunities Over-dependency on others Severe emotional stresses Feeling overwhelmed by burdens of others
GREEN	Emotional confusion Lack of clear insight and understanding Feelings of anger Lack of emotional stability
BLUE-GREEN (teal)	Lack of hope Lack of faith Feelings of bewilderment Need for more optimism
LIGHT BLUE	Mental dullness Inability to see clearly Lack of practicality Indecisiveness
DARK BLUE	Fear of the unknown Identity crisis Inability to accept a leadership position Nervousness and fear of travelling
MAUVE	Feeling fatigued from talking Need for emotional relaxation Lack of intuitive awareness Minimising phobias
PURPLE	Feelings of inferiority Lack of inner peace Guilt feelings Excessive worry about imaginary problems

BROWN	Emotional insecurity Lack of physical stamina Uncertainties about future Fear of survival
BLACK	Need for extra emotional protection Supersensitivity to the environment Over-responsiveness to emotional stresses Fear of being taken advantage of
WHITE	Excessive worry or mental confusion Need for extra spiritual protection Fear of bad-habit addiction Need for more time and freedom
GREY	Overwhelming feelings of stress Fear of invasion of privacy Emotional over-involvements Mental fatigue
SILVER	Distrust of others Poor self-image Decreased self-worth Feelings of not performing satisfactorily
GOLD	Feelings of continuous victimisation Lack of better goal opportunities Fear of accomplishment of success Insecurity concerning material gain

I have received many wonderful letters attesting to the power of colour as an agent for attitude change, and how colour has worked to aid people coping with the stresses of life. I would like to share a few of these with you.

(Letter 1 – from a municipal employee, a social worker)

Dear Dottee,

I wanted to let you know how much I appreciate your support and insight and how helpful the SICA and my attitude support colours were for me last month, during the difficult time after my husband's death. I am feeling better and I have come to feel very grateful for the colour, yellow, that you suggested I wear when depressed.

Each time when I found myself dwelling on the past and feeling sorry for myself, I put on my yellow blouse or sweater. I felt better and am grateful for the knowledge of how colour can help one to cope. My husband also used his colours when he needed to shrug off heartache or loneliness. I like to think that they were helpful to him during his last days of life.

(Letter 2 – from a high school principal)

Dear Dottee:

With your consultation, our high school has started to come alive with beautiful colours that are inspiring pride and creativity in our staff and students. During the years numerous classrooms and offices have been painted voluntarily by students, teachers and office personnel. Our custodians are also voluntarily doing the graphic work in our hallways, and their excellent work has received much notice and praise.

As principal of the school, I have received accolades that I want to share with you. Many positive responses regarding the improved appearance and attitude of the students continually come from parents, staff members, and visitors to our school.

My gratitude goes to you for your expert assistance. Henry J. Kaiser once said, 'When your work speaks for itself, don't interrupt.' As I walk these halls, your work (colours) speaks. Many thanks.

(Letter 3– from a personnel administrator of a large factory)

Dear Dottee:
It was fun to evaluate and coordinate my wardrobe to help me present myself in my best colours. They have indeed helped my attitude. Here at work I've noticed that my colleagues are 'sprucing up', not only the ladies but the men too. I'm sure that my SICA has rubbed off on them. Because I now understand 'my' particular colours, I wear my clothes with new assurance.

I've also gained more inner awareness. The SICA gave me many insights regarding not only myself, but also into other people as well. The wearing of the right colour at the right time has aided my attitude immensely.

Thank you again for a most rewarding experience. Hopefully, depending on next year's budget, other employees will be taking your SICA in the future.

(Letter 4 – from a church programme director)

Dear Dottee:
Our church has a new colour scheme, new stained-glass windows, and a new attitude thanks to your work in selecting colours for the sanctuary and other areas of the church building. It's hard to believe that just a year ago our building had the same 'ordinary' colours found in most churches. However, as soon as the sanctuary was painted in colours that you suggested, the minister and congregation decided that it was time to create a new set of windows.

Within three months an artist had been commissioned to design a unique set of windows depicting the major religions of the world, the stained glass had been installed, and most importantly, the congregation had raised the entire $13,000 cost of the windows. During this time the church also redecorated the fellowship hall, remodelled the entrance area, painted the entire outside of the building, and generally gave the place the 'face-lift' that was needed.

In addition a to the new colours and new paint, there is a feeling of commitment and community that did not exist last year, which I attribute to the changes in the physical surroundings. This is now a church that people are proud of and excited about. I feel that your initial assistance with colours set us on the right track as we fulfil our spiritual purpose.

These letters attest to the helpful support that colour has given to many in various professional fields. Colour acted as an agent of support and change to the routine stresses of life. Whether it was placed on a wall or used as a natural support in the wardrobe, the result was the same – a knowledgeable use of colour answered the need.

8

Colour and Its Association with the Healing Arts

THE history of colour is interlaced with early pioneers in healing and science. From ancient Egypt and the isles of Greece to the Italian peninsula and the city of Rome, colour was spoken as one of the languages for health. Pythagoras, Hermes, Hippocrates, Democritus, Aristotle, and Galen, just to mention a few, all gave credibility to colour as an 'outward expression' of an internal pathological condition. Although centuries apart, the physicians Pythagoras in Greece and Galen in Rome treated with colours. Pythagoras was reported to have used colour and music to cure disease, while Galen believed that external application of colour could encourage the healing of an internal condition. Hippocrates, the renowned physician who wrote the oath that all medical doctors follow today, found that the colour of a patient's skin determined the condition of their health. His theory was that a flushed or reddened skin indicated circulatory disease, a yellow appearance gave the sign of stomach or liver involvement, and blue to black discolouration of the body showed a terminal illness. He prescribed many treatments and medicines based on his diagnostic attitude towards skin discolouration.

But if I could retravel the avenues of time, the physician that

I would enjoy meeting today would be the eleventh-century Persian Islamic philosopher and healer Avicenna – the father of colour therapy. Far, far from Rome and Greece, this passionate man influenced all of Europe. Not only did he use colour for diagnosis, but also as a cure. In his *Canon of Medicine* he gave credit to colour as a most important curative; he even wrapped his patients in red bandages to stimulate their circulation for healing. Avicenna was known throughout Europe for his red cloak, which he wore as a physician's mantle. In a later era, English physicians copied his attire, but sadly not his example of healing. Hundreds of years passed before colour therapy again became recognised as a treatment for illness.

Colour healing surfaced again in later nineteenth-century America due to the efforts of Edwin D. Babbitt, a mystic, artist, and physician. Like Avicenna, Dr Babbit expounded upon the relationship between colour and medicine. In his journal, *The Principles of Light and Colour*, published in 1878, he chose the three primaries – red, yellow, and blue – as the basic healing rays of colour. He felt that each colour had an opposite colour that affected the return of balance to the body. For example, if a person was reacting over-emotionally (red), he would expose them to a treatment of green light, which would calm their emotions and bring them back to balance. Although much of his research was discounted by the medical profession, his theories are being re-examined today and their intrinsic value is being recognised.

This chapter will deal specifically with the wearing of colours as personal resources to aid health. Art therapies have attempted to explore and explain the emotional significance of colour and form. Not much information is available on the wearing of colours to aid certain problems. Some therapists feel that the excessive use of black in the wardrobe indicates negative qualities, but as yet this too has not been scientifically proven. Black, however, isn't all bad, for it might be used as a positive colour if one is wearing it to protect a sensitive nature.

Creatively, you, as your own self-healer, can use the electro-magnetic energy of colour to give you added support to help you on your way back to health. We, as human beings, emanate energy fields, discovered and named 'corona discharges' in 1939 by the Soviet photographer-scientist Semyon Kirlian. The world revealed by these 'radiation field photographs' showed that plant leaves, coins, jewellery, and human appendages were all surrounded by 'halos' of energy. Invisible to the human eye, vibrations of energy swirl around and out from us, like 'reaching out' hands or antennae. Recognise the love feelings or electric energy that you receive from another, or the magnetism of a famous personality filling a room with their presence; all exemplify this movement of energy.

Many great European painters of the past, such as the early Italian art masters Fra Angelico and Giotto, along with other well-known 'halo' artists, have attempted to portray these human rainbows. None painted them the same, not in shape, size, or form, but all visualised them as extensions of the human body. For those of you who are into the New Age philosophies, you already comprehend that we have an energy body as well as a physical one. Both react to all outside stimulants. Those early sensitive artists did indeed paint the auras, and futurists for tomorrow project that science will be exploring them for clues to health. This chapter will help you to understand how your energy fields respond to colour.

Colours react and interact with your vibrations to balance, weaken, or support. When you hurt or want a natural Band-Aid for relief, the energy of a colour might just be the thing to help.

Following is a chart to guide you in the use of colour application or the wearing of colours for natural healing support. Not all this information is, as yet, documented by science and research. Yet, around the country, many re-searchers into natural therapies are trying colours for healing. Without waiting for scientific approval, these practitioners of the healing arts are using colours for their soothing and beneficial effects. 'Colour support has improved countless clients' health and resistance to stress, combined with balanced nutrition and exercises,' writes Michelle Lusson in her book, *Creative Wellness, A Holistic Guide to Total Health*. These and other statements are gradually increasing the public's awareness that colour does help.

COLOURS FOR HEALTH SUPPORT

Colour	Good for:	Not Good for:
RED	Upper or lower backache Colds and flus All sprains and muscle disorders Healing of burns	Coronary diseases (May use blue-greens)
PINK	Heart spasms or angina Circulatory problems Blood disorders Asthmas	Weight problems (May use dark blue)
MAROON	Female disorders (such as cramps) Stiff necks Complexion problems Aching or cold feet	Thyroid dysfunctions (May use peach)
ORANGE	Arthritis or joint stiffness Constipation Stiff joints Lower-back aches	Hyperactivity Alcoholism (May use light blues)

Colour	Good for:	Not Good For:

PEACH	Dieting
	Lower-bowel
	  problems
	Digestive disorders
		Headaches
		(May use light
		  purples)

YELLOW	Adrenal weakness
	Bladder or kidney
	Mental depression
	Food allergies
		Drug addiction or
		  liver/gall bladder
		  disorders
		(May use browns)

MINT GREEN	Fevers Stomach-aches Infections Sinus problems	Adrenal weakness or stress prevention (May use maroon)
GREEN	High blood pressure Colitis or diarrhoea Eye problems Weight problems	Allergies (May use golds or deep yellows)

LIGHT BLUE	Sunburn
	Fluid retention
	  problems
	Sore throats
	Hyperactivity
		Insomnia or
		  sleeping
		  problems
		Mental stress
		(May use deep
		  pinks)

DARK BLUE	Leg spasms
	Thyroid disorders
	Impaired smell or
	  taste
	Physical
	  coordination
	  problems
		Lung problems
		(May use pale
		  yellows)

Colour	Good for:	Not Good For:

PURPLE	Headaches
	Addictions
	Sleep problems
	Sexual
	  over-stimulation
		Female disorders
		  especially cramps
		(May use reds)

BROWN	Weight loss
	Hypoglycaemia or
	  diabetes
	Female hormone
	  imbalance
	Bone structure
	  weakness
		Lower-bowel
		  problems
		(May use peach)

BLACK	Muscular weakness
	Over-active glandular
	  function
	Nervousness
	  (excessive)
		Depression or
		  moodiness
		(May use yellows)

GREY	Muscular tensions
	Stress-related
	  illnesses
	Poor digestion and
	  bloating
	Inflammation and
	  swelling
		Lower-back aches
		(May use maroon)

WHITE	Itching
	Dermatitis or heat
	  rash
	Muscular spasms
	Earaches
		Digestive disorders
		(May use peach or
		  blue-greens)

9

Share the Language of Colour

AS new methods of satellite communication bridge the continents of the world, colour and its emanations are becoming a medium of universal exchange. SICA is the lexicon or grammar of the language of colour, a new form of non-verbal communication. Some of you have already discovered your personal sensitivity to the hues of the rainbow, while others, desiring to know more about themselves, are still testing their inner feelings for colours. SICA is one of those new forms of non-verbal communications. For those of you who like self-analysing methods, SICA is now for you an uncomplicated tool for self-portrait visualisation. It will always be easy to administer as it is fun, as straightforward as saying hello – no more complex than a child's colouring book.

The art students who helped design it discovered that SICA motivated and inspired them to reach out for new horizons and the fulfilment of their dreams. For its colour message alone, many people have utilised their SICA self-portrait to improve their personal and professional relationships. It can also be used as a personal image and design counsellor for getting the most power out of yourself. When you're at odds with yourself, or you just need that extra boost, your colours can return you to balance naturally.

I hope that with the book you have found a new method to heighten your awareness of your talents through the language of colour, and the use of your personal colours. It has also been my intent to show how colour itself, a natural energy, can give you support – even physical support – better communications, and most important, a new intuitive insight into yourself. Share it with another!

Bibliography

Babbit, Edwin D. *The Principles of Light and Colour*. Published originally in 1878, East Orange, NJ: by the author. Currently reprinted by Citadel Press, Secaucus, NJ.

Birren, Faber. *Colour, A Survey in Words and Pictures, From Ancient Mysticism to Modern Science*. Secaucus, NJ: University Books, 1963.

Gruner, O. Cameron. *A Treatise on the Canon of Medicine of Avicenna*. London: Luzac & Co, 1930

Jackson, Carole. *Colour Me Beautiful*. New York: Ballantine Books, 1981.

Kandinsky, Wassily. *The Art of Spiritual Harmony*. Boston: Houghton Mifflin Co., 1914.

Luscher, Dr Max. *The Luscher Colour Test*. New York: Pocket Books, 1969.

Lusson, Michelle. *Creative Wellness, A Holistic Guide to Total Health*. New York: Warner Books, 1987.

The Rainbow Book. Edited by F. Lanier Graham. New York: Vintage Books, division of Random House, NY, 1979.

The writings and philosophies of these pioneers in the field of colour and colour research inspired me in my work to synthesise my theories into practical applications, but most important, to remain true to my beliefs – **colour is a universal language**.

Index